Storytime Mathtime

Math Explorations in Children's Literature

Patricia Satariano

Dale Seymour Publications

Dedication

To all my students, whose needs inspired this book.

Managing Editor: Michael Kane

Senior Editor: Priscilla Cox Samii

Production/Mfg Director: Janet Yearian

Production/Mfg Coordinator: Leanne Collins

Design Manager: Jeff Kelly

Illustrations: Rachel Gage

Cover Design: Rachel Gage

Text Design: Paula Shuhert

This book is published by Dale Seymour Publications, an imprint of the Alternative Publishing Group of Addison-Wesley.

Order number DS21223

ISBN 0-86651-732-4

This book is printed
on recycled paper.

DALE
SEYMOUR
PUBLICATIONS
P.O. BOX 10888
PALO ALTO, CA 94303

1 2 3 4 5 6 7 8 9 10-ML-98 97 96 95 94 93

Contents

Introduction

Teaching has changed greatly in recent years, and meeting all the educational needs of students has become more difficult than ever. There isn't enough time in the teaching day to address all the changes in the curriculum. The math explorations I offer in this book are designed to help you integrate mathematics into your literature program. They are meant to be an addition to your math program. The explorations will increase your students' mathematical language and communication skill, introduce them to a variety of strategies, and engage them in problems that require persistence rather than quick reaction. The goal is to help students become mathematically powerful.

The explorations in *Storytime, Mathtime* are based on teachers' and children's favorite stories. Some of the titles are classics: *Caps for Sale* by Esphyr Slobodkina, *Corduroy* by Don Freeman, and *Millions of Cats* by Wanda Gág. I have also included some new favorites, such as *The Grouchy Ladybug* by Eric Carle, *A Chair for My Mother* by Vera B. Williams, and *The Relatives Came* by Cynthia Rylant. *Storytime, Mathtime* includes 67 math explorations based on 18 children's books. Each exploration is the result of many experiences with students from grades 1–3. There is no set sequence for using the explorations. I have used an exploration to introduce a storybook as well as to extend the initial reading of the book. I have taken the same storybook and explorations to an older class and found students were delighted to visit with an old friend. The depth of understanding of the mathematical concept will vary from age group to age group.

Finding Math Explorations in Children's Literature

Many of the teachers who have used these math explorations expressed greater understanding of the changes in content and approach in the math curriculum. They began to see the potential integration possibilities in other storybooks. Use *Storytime, Mathtime* as a guide. Feel free to adapt any lesson to meet your individual needs or those of your students. I have taken the same lesson into three different classes in one day and had three different experiences. You must be prepared to be a facilitator who guides with probing questions and gentle suggestions and who recognizes when a new direction is necessary. Stress the language development and communication factors in every exploration. If you are going to extend the lessons in a center, do so only after you have introduced the initial lesson with the entire class. Many of the explorations are introductions to problem-solving strategies and must be modeled. Whole-class presentations provide opportunities to monitor students' thinking, introduce mathematical language, and assess the effectiveness of your program.

The explorations will also enable you to incorporate math with literature that is compatible with mathematical investigations. The first story that I based a math exploration on was "A Lost Button" from *Frog and Toad Are Friends* by Arnold Lobel. I brought my collection of buttons to school to accompany the reading of the story. Students started grouping the buttons and discussing their attributes without any direction from me. I had become a facilitator of learning without even trying. Exploring attributes and developing language with buttons was so successful that I started looking at every storybook in a new way.

After using these explorations and becoming more familiar with math content areas, you will start to recognize storybooks suited for this type of integration. On page 160 is a list of additional storybooks that I have found to be suitable for math explorations. I have also included a Resource Bibliography (page 158) that contains books that have been helpful to me in gaining a greater knowledge of the changes in math instruction.

Using the Storybooks

Before beginning a set of explorations, have students read the related storybook. Many students will have read the book before but will enjoy reading it again. If you have nonreaders among your students, read the book to them. Then review the story characters and events with students to make sure they understand the storyline.

Why a Change in Content and Approach?

My approach grows from a national reform of the mathematics curriculum. Many teachers and districts throughout the country have recognized the need to emphasize problem solving and hands-on, interactive learning that includes all the strands of mathematics to promote mathematical power. The National Council of Teachers of Mathematics (NCTM) published *Curriculum and Evaluation Standards for School Mathematics* in 1989 in response to efforts to identify both the content and evaluation necessary for a successful mathematics curriculum. The *Standards* were established to set goals, ensure quality, and promote change. The identified areas of emphasis include Number, Geometry, Measurement, Logic, Mathematical Language, Estimation, Problem Solving, Patterns, Probability, and Statistics. Students must be prepared to be mathematically literate so that they can function successfully in our information society. To accomplish this, the *Standards* lists five general goals for all students.

Students will:

- value mathematics
- become confident in their mathematical ability
- become mathematical problem solvers
- communicate mathematically
- reason mathematically

These goals have necessitated a change of emphasis in teaching approach as well as in content.

New Areas of Emphasis

Mathematical Language

Language is the connector that helps students construct links from concrete materials to the abstract language and symbolism of math. It is important to provide opportunities for students to communicate their knowledge and reasoning. Students will learn new strategies, clarify their thinking, and develop a deeper understanding from group discussions. End every exploration with a verbal sharing to assess student comprehension and to give students an opportunity to learn from each other. Written summations are especially beneficial to those students who are reluctant to share verbally. Ways in which young mathematicians can record the results of an exploration include written accounts, simple diagrams, and math journals.

The Teacher's Role

The teacher's first aim is to foster a supportive classroom atmosphere, where every student's thinking is valued and where ample time and materials are available for engaging explorations. Instead of referring to your lesson plans to decide on the length of an exploration, observe the attention level of your class. Are students still engaged? Are they discussing, sharing, testing? Ask questions that stimulate their curiosity and require critical thinking. Don't always rescue them with specific direction; sometimes it's best to let them discover their own mistakes. It is important to empower students by providing the skills it takes to become responsible, individual thinkers. Diversify your teaching with whole-class, small-group, and individual instruction. Weave the mathematical areas into units of varying length and depth. Build your assessment of students and your program into the explorations. I learn as much from my failures as I do from successful lessons, and thoughtful introspection has often redirected my approach or goals for a lesson. In the middle of an exploration with a small group of first graders that was obviously not engaging the students, I asked them to think about how they would change the rules of the game. They came up with a more developmentally appropriate sequence for the exploration. I sat back, watched, and listened to students who were learning.

Authentic Assessment

We hear a lot about *authentic assessment*. The term refers to looking at what students can actually do with the information they have learned. It provides the teacher with a window into students' thinking and the success of the math program. Assessment should give students a direction to improve the quality of their work. Good assessment goes hand in hand with learning by helping students judge the quality of their own work. Some perspectives to keep in mind when planning authentic assessments include:

- The work and the assessment are simultaneous.
- The conditions do not change during assessment. Students should have sufficient time, tools, and communication opportunities to reach conclusions.
- Students should not be assessed when being introduced to a new exploration format.
- Tasks should be meaningful and diversified.
- Assessment should also evaluate the math program to determine whether activities are developmentally suitable.
- Students need to feel involved in the assessment process. A student needs to recognize quality work and to understand how to revise until that goal is reached.

- There are a variety of assessment techiques: open-ended investigations, student portfolios, and direct observation of students at work.

Mathematical Power

The *Mathematics Framework for California Public Schools*, which supports the NCTM *Standards*, establishes the goal of mathematical power for all students. "Mathematically powerful students think and communicate, drawing on mathematical ideas and using mathematical tools and techniques." (*Mathematics Framework for California Public Schools*, 1992, page 3)

A program that develops mathematically powerful students will:

- **encourage students to think.** We want to foster the higher-order thinking skills, such as classifying, planning, investigating, verifying, and evaluating.
- **encourage students to communicate.** Mathematical communication should be diversified with class discussions, individual presentations, written summaries, diagrams, charts, graphs, and numerical expressions.
- **encourage students to use mathematical ideas.** In order to become mathematically literate, students must have a working knowledge of measurement, geometry, statistics, probability, logic, and patterns, as well as arithmetic. All of these areas should be experienced in a developmentally appropriate curriculum. A sound mathematical foundation is created through many enjoyable contacts with integrated concepts rather than through presentation of isolated skills.
- **encourage students to choose an appropriate tool or technique.** Manipulative materials should be available so that students can explore concepts. Counters, cubes, pattern blocks, Base Ten Blocks, geoboards, spinners, balances, and graph paper are some of the many options. Estimation is another tool that needs to be included in a student's earliest mathematical experiences. When a student uses a calculator without a background in esti-

mation, the results are often grossly inaccurate. Students need to be able to recognize when they have entered the wrong numbers or process keys.

Provide your students many opportunities to use a variety of strategies. Discuss the effectiveness of specific strategies in solving particular problems. Generate a list of the strategies that you introduce to students, such as: draw a picture, use counters, guess and check, simplify, use a chart or table, and look for a pattern.

Summary

I hope you and your students enjoy the explorations in *Storytime, Mathtime*. I encourage you to personalize the explorations—adapt them to meet your unique teaching style. Let's make math a time for discussion, building, testing, recording, and, above all, persistence.

Books Selected for *Storytime, Mathtime*

Allen, Pamela. *Who Sank the Boat?* Coward-McCann, 1982.

Barrett, Judi. *Cloudy with a Chance of Meatballs.* Atheneum, 1978.

Burningham, John. *Mr. Gumpy's Outing.* Holt, Rinehart and Winston, 1970.

Carle, Eric. *The Grouchy Ladybug.* Crowell Junior Books, 1977; Harper Trophy Picture Books, 1986.

de Paola, Tomie. *Strega Nona.* Prentice Hall, 1975.

Gág, Wanda. *Millions of Cats.* Coward-McCann, 1928; Sandcastle Books, 1988.

Freeman, Don. *Corduroy.* Viking, 1968; Puffin, 1976.

Keller, Holly. *Geraldine's Blanket.* Greenwillow Books, 1984.

Hutchins, Pat. *The Doorbell Rang.* Greenwillow Books, 1986.

Lobel, Arnold. *Frog and Toad Are Friends.* Harper & Row, 1970.

Martin, Bill, Jr., and John Archambault. *Knots on a Counting Rope.* Henry Holt and Company, 1987.

Rey, H. A. *Curious George Rides a Bike.* Houghton Mifflin, 1952.

Rylant, Cynthia. *The Relatives Came.* Bradbury Press, 1985.

Slobodkina, Esphyr. *Caps for Sale.* Harper & Row Junior Books, 1987.

Tompert, Ann. *Grandfather Tang's Story.* Crown Publishers, 1990.

Walsh, Ellen Stoll. *Mouse Count.* Harcourt Brace Jovanovich, 1991.

Williams, Vera B. *A Chair for My Mother.* Greenwillow Books, 1982.

Williams, Vera B. *Cherries and Cherry Pits.* Greenwillow Books, 1986.

MATH EXPLORATIONS BASED ON

Mouse Count

by Ellen Stoll Walsh

• •

Ten field mice find themselves in a predicament—they are about to become the next meal of a very hungry snake. Fortunately for them, the snake is also a very greedy snake.

Explorations	Areas of Emphasis
Is It 10 Yet?	Number Logic
Make a Snake	Measurement: linear Number Statistics: graphing
Mouse Groups	Number Problem Solving Mathematical Language

Mouse Count
by Ellen Stoll Walsh

Is It 10 Yet?

Areas of Emphasis

- Number
- Logic

Group Size

- Pairs of students

Teacher Materials

- mouse counters and 10-strip master (page 3)

Student Materials

For each pair

- mouse counters and 10-strip
- tape

Introduction

Say: "We are going to learn how to play a game that you will play with a partner. The object of the game is to be the one who puts the tenth mouse on the strip." Before beginning the game, give each pair of students a copy of the mouse counters and 10-strip sheet. Have them cut out the counters and then cut out and tape together the two parts of the ten-strip.

Procedure

Model the game with a student first. Explain the rules:

- You can put only one or two mice on the strip at a time. Whether you put one or two is up to you.
- Your goal is to be the one who puts the tenth mouse on the strip.
- If you get to ten first, make a tally mark on a piece of paper.
- Continue playing the game with your partner, taking turns going first.
- The person who gets five tally marks first wins the round.

If students haven't used tally marks before, give each pair a "score card." Tell them to mark over the light tally marks on the score card to keep score.

Have the materials available so that students can play after the initial instruction. Encourage them to play with different partners. This is a good independent activity to use once students have learned the format. After students have played several times, ask them if they have developed a winning strategy. Tell them to write about their strategy in their math journals.

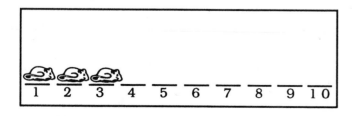

I learnd there are patterns in games and I learnd how to play the game Mouse Count. in Mouse count I learned to see how the other people would win and I would win.

Mouse Count
by Ellen Stoll Walsh

Mouse Counters and 10-Strip

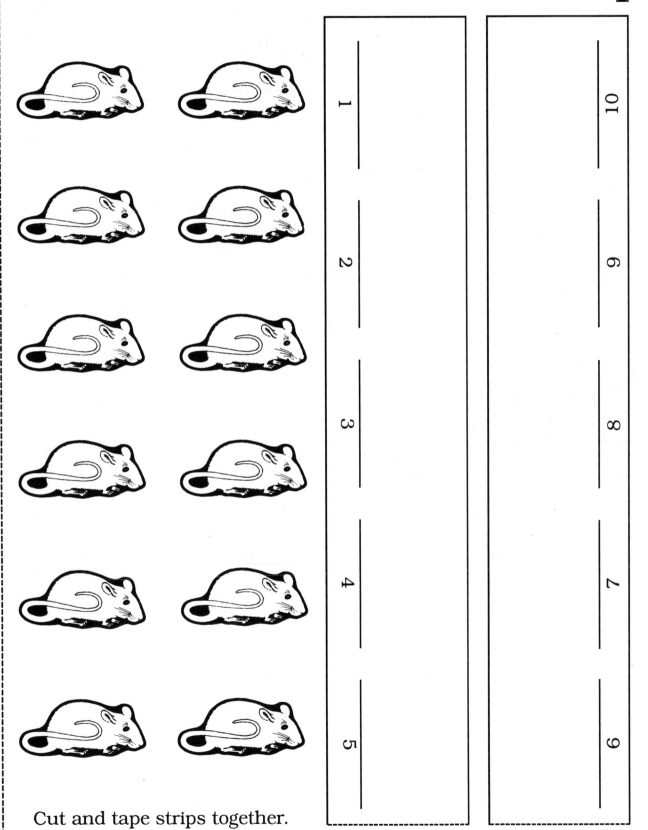

Cut and tape strips together.

Make a Snake

Areas of Emphasis

- Measurement: linear
- Number
- Statistics: graphing

Group Size

- Individuals in pairs

Teacher Materials

- 5-foot sheet of butcher paper
- stick of clay
- penny or other item to be used as a nonstandard measuring unit (e.g., paper clip, pasta, button)

Student Materials

For each student
- 5-foot sheet of butcher paper (per pair)
- stick of clay
- penny or other nonstandard measuring unit
- craft stick (optional)

Introduction

Actually measuring things in order to compare or gain knowledge about them is the best way to teach these skills. Students should first use appropriate nonstandard units for measuring. Say: "Let's make our own snakes. I am going to give each of you a stick of clay. You will roll it out until you have made a snake. Then we will compare our snakes." Set aside a table or section of floor for this activity. You will be surprised how long some of the snakes will get. They are pretty fragile when they get very thin, so don't count on moving them for a while.

Procedure

This is an individual activity that is best managed in pairs. Assign pairs of students to one sheet of butcher paper. Instruct them each to roll out a snake and then measure it with a nonstandard unit of measurement. I have found that pennies work very well. They are easy to flip over, and they make clear indentions on the clay. I recommend having students make a notation on the paper alongside the snake every 5 or 10 units. Model the entire process for the class before students begin.

When everyone has finished, have students compare the "penny lengths" of their snakes. Have them write their names and snake lengths on pieces of paper. Tape the papers on the chalkboard, arranged from smallest to longest snake length.

Discuss the measuring process. Say: "Was it important that we all used a penny to measure our snakes? We all started out with the same amount of clay. Why were our snakes different lengths?"

Kristyn 43   Ryan 44   Melissa 45   Yoshi 47   Ben 48

Extensions

- Say: "Yoshi's snake was 47 pennies long. How many nickels would you get for 47 pennies?" Using either pennies and nickels or beans and portion cups, solve this first exchange problem together. Then let the partners solve the rest of the penny-length exchanges.

- Tell students that an easy way to compare the various snake lengths is to put the information on a graph. A graph tells the clearest story without many words. You will have to set the graph up for students. Have them write their name and then fill in the correct number of blocks in their column to correspond to their snake's penny length. Discuss the advantages of having this information on a graph.

- Have students use a longer unit, such as a craft stick, to measure the snakes. Ask: "How many craft-stick lengths will your snake be?" Record students' estimates and then have them check their predictions.

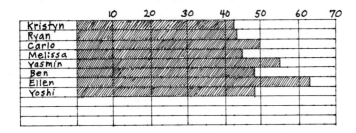

Mouse Groups

Areas of Emphasis

- Number
- Problem Solving
- Mathematical Language

Group Size

- Pairs of students

Teacher Materials

- mouse counters master (page 7)
- jar picture master (page 8)

Student Materials

For each pair

- 10 mouse counters
- jar picture

Introduction

Say: "There are mice in the jar and mice out of the jar. Sometimes there are more mice in the jar than outside. At other times, there are more mice outside the jar than in the jar. We are going to find all the possible situations. You can record your findings in a table or in a picture. We'll do one situation together."

Procedure

Divide the class into pairs. Give each pair ten mice counters, a jar picture, and paper. Pairs should work together to find all the possible groupings for the mice. Do the first possibility with the class. Say: "There is one mouse in the jar. How many mice are not in the jar?" Then tell students to record this combination on their paper. Let them share their different recording techniques. When students understand the procedure, tell them to find all the other possible groupings for ten mice in and out of the jar.

Extension

Have students divide the ten mice into three groups: inside the jar, outside the jar, and at home. Again, the recording technique is their decision. Ask: "Why did you decide on that recording technique? Did you use a pattern to get all the possibilities?"

Mouse Counters

Jar

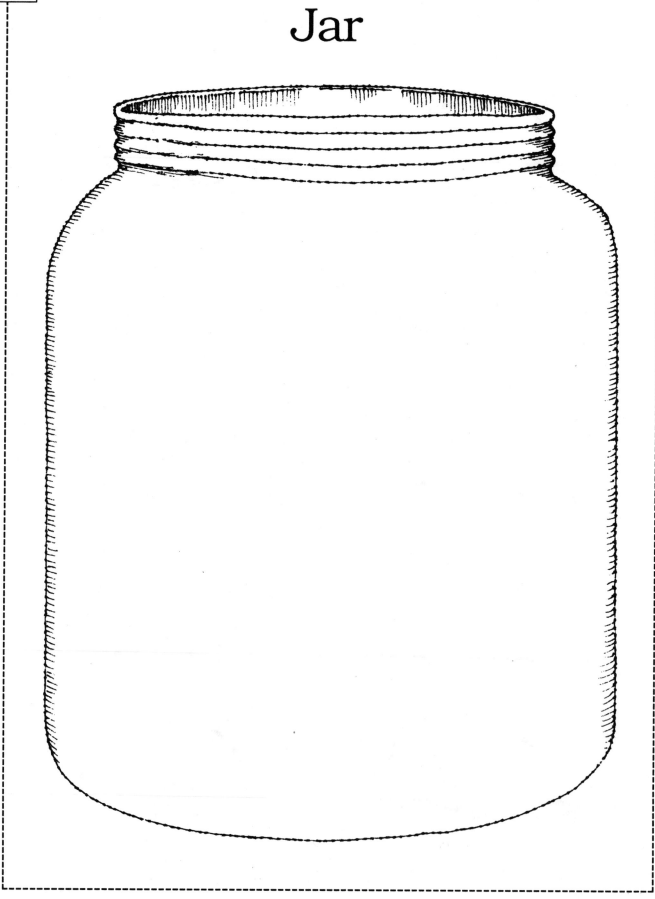

MATH EXPLORATIONS BASED ON

Geraldine's Blanket

by Holly Keller

• •

Geraldine loved the blanket that she'd had since she was a baby. But as Geraldine got older, so did the blanket, and her parents wanted her to give it up. In the end, Geraldine comes up with an inspired and creative solution to the problem.

Explorations	Areas of Emphasis
Rebuilding a Blanket	Geometry Mathematical Language
Tangram Cut-Ups	Geometry Mathematical Language
The Patch	Geometry Logic

Rebuilding a Blanket

Areas of Emphasis

- Geometry
- Mathematical Language

Group Size

- 4–6 students

Teacher Materials

- a variety of 8-inch wallpaper or colored paper squares
- scissor

Student Materials

For each group

- 8-inch wallpaper or colored paper squares
- scissors
- glue

Introduction

Say: "I admire Geraldine. She practices recycling! I also admire her because she is a problem solver. She found a solution to her problem. We are going to do an exploration today that Geraldine would admire."

Procedure

Divide the class into small groups of 4–6 students. Let each student choose a wallpaper square or a piece of colored paper. The lesson will be more successful if everyone has a different pattern or color. Have students iron out this first potential problem in their groups. Remind them that Geraldine would find a solution!

Tell students they are going to divide up their blanket and share parts of it with their groupmates. Instruct them to fold the square of paper in half and cut along the fold line. Ask: "What do we have now?" This is the time to develop appropriate mathematical language: rectangles, equal pieces, halves. Involve the entire class in the discussion. Say: "Take one of the rectangles and fold it in half again. Cut carefully along the fold line. What do you have now? Can you put these pieces back into a big square again? How are the rectangle and the squares the same? How are they different?"

Continue by having students fold one of the squares in half and cut along the fold line. They now have one large rectangle, two smaller rectangles, and one square. Have them discuss, share, and rebuild the pieces to make a large square. Then tell them to fold both small rectangles in half and cut. Again begin a class discussion. Ask: "What do you have now? How are the big square and the small squares the same? Can you put the pieces into the square we started with? Can you make one big rectangle with the pieces?"

This is an appropriate place to stop if your lesson has gone beyond your time limits or the students' attention span. The length of an exploration differs from class to class. I have gone into four different classes with the same lesson outline and seldom got the same results. Your class will dictate the flow of the lesson. A successful exploration depends on your flexibility. If you need to stop, have students store the shapes in an envelope with their name on it.

To continue the lesson, bring the same group members together. Tell them to put all their pieces back into a square first. For some, this will be a difficult task. Next, ask them to trade a piece of their blanket with someone in their group. They may continue trading until they are happy with their new blankets. One of my students renamed the blankets "friendship blankets." Students will soon realize how important it is to trade pieces of equal shape and size. This is a good opportunity to discuss the concept of area.

Extensions

■ Have students build new blankets using squares, triangles, and rectangles. Let them fold and cut until they want to stop. Ask: "Who has the most triangles? Whose blanket has the most parts? Who has the most squares?" Students may trade pieces of equal shape and size. This is an open-ended exploration that students will enjoy.

■ Say: "Suppose you have a square that measures four inches on each side. If you fold and cut it in half, what will you have? How long will the sides be?" Encourage students to use any mathematical tools they need: pictures, models, rulers, and so on.

Tangram Cut-Ups

Areas of Emphasis

- Geometry
- Mathematical Language

Group Size

- 3–4 students

Teacher Materials

- tangram master (page 13)
- glue
- butcher paper

Student Materials

For each group

- drawing paper (per student)
- crayons (per student)
- tangram sets (2 or more sets)
- scissors
- glue

Introduction

Ask: "Did you have a favorite blanket when you were a small child? Do you remember what it looked like?" I predict an enthusiastic discussion. In one of my classes, many students brought in their baby blankets. They related some interesting reminiscences during sharing and sat with their blankets during storytime.

Supply each student with a piece of drawing paper and crayons. Their assignment is to draw the pattern and color of their blanket. If they did not have a blanket or can't remember what it looked like, they may design a blanket.

Procedure

Before the lesson, make multiple copies of the tangram master on page 13 and glue them onto cardboard for strength and durability. Cut out the tangram pieces and store each set in a self-lock plastic bag.

Divide the class into small groups of three or four students. Supply each group with at least two tangram sets. Say: "A tangram is an ancient Chinese puzzle. It has seven pieces that make up a square. You can make many designs, animals, people, and letters from these seven pieces. Trace all the tangram pieces carefully on your blanket." Laminate the drawings if possible before students cut the pieces out.

Have students explore the tangram blanket pieces, using them to create different designs. Encourage them to challenge each other. Say: "I made a rabbit from my blanket pieces. Can anyone else?" Let students share their designs as they make them. "Which letters of the alphabet can you make?" When interest has diminished, ask students to put the pieces into their favorite design. Glue the design on a square piece of paper. Arrange and glue all the squares on a large piece of butcher paper to create a class blanket.

Extension

Supply math centers with tangram sets. Challenge students with various tasks. Say: "Can you make a square using six pieces? Can you make any rectangles? How many different shapes can you make with the three smallest triangles? Trace the shape to record it."

Tangram

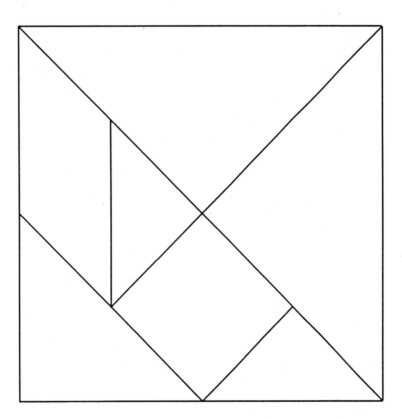

The Patch

Areas of Emphasis

- Geometry
- Logic

Group Size

- Individuals

Teacher Materials

- red trapezoids and green triangles (pattern blocks or corresponding paper shapes)
- recording sheet master (page 15)

Student Materials

For each student

- 2 red trapezoids and 4 green triangles (pattern blocks or corresponding paper shapes)
- recording sheet
- crayons

Introduction

Say: "Geraldine's blanket was getting so worn out that it needed to be mended. Geraldine made a very interesting patch outline. Using material saved from her favorite old dresses, she cut out some shapes. Help her piece the shapes on the patch outline. She knows that there is more than one way to arrange the shapes. She suspects that there are many. She's right!"

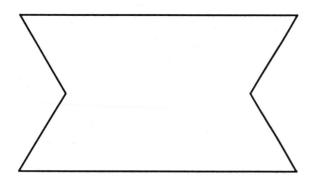

Procedure

This is an individual exploration. Each student should have two red trapezoids, four green triangles, and a recording sheet. If you do not have enough pattern blocks for the class, paper pieces work well also. Every time a student finds a new way to fill the patch, it should be drawn on the recording sheet so that students can check to see if they have duplicated a design.

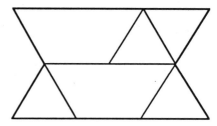

Encourage students to be persistent. My students found over 15 different ways to fill in the patch. They even took the recording sheets and pattern pieces home.

Extensions

- Have students make a graph of the solutions. Ask: "Which solution was discovered most often? Which was discovered least often?"
- Have students make a different patch outline using the trapezoids and triangles and record the results.

Recording Sheet

Name _____

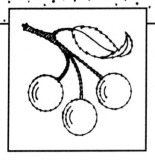

Cherries and Cherry Pits

by Vera B. Williams

• •

This is a story of a little girl named Bidemmi. She loves to draw and tell wonderfully rich stories about people. All the stories involve cherries, cherry pits, and love.

Explorations	Areas of Emphasis
Cherry Trees	Patterns
	Number
	Geometry
Mismatch	Mathematical Language
	Number

Cherry Trees

Areas of Emphasis

- Patterns
- Number
- Geometry

Group Size

- Individuals in small groups

Student Materials

For each student

- brown, green, and red construction paper
- scissors
- envelope
- paste
- black marker

Introduction

Have students trace and cut the shapes necessary to make cherry trees: one 2" x 6" brown rectangle and several ½" x 3" brown rectangles for the trunk and branches; 2" x 2" x 2" green triangles for the leaves; and 1" diameter red circles for the cherries. Have students store the shapes in an envelope with their name on it.

Say: "Bidemmi creates a forest of cherry trees on her block with the magic of her pens. We are going to create a forest of cherry trees for our classroom bulletin board."

Procedure

This is an individual project that is easily managed in small groups. Say: "Paste the shapes on your paper to make a cherry tree. The large rectangle can be the trunk, the small rectangles can be branches, and the triangles can be leaves. The circles are the cherries. Put the cherries on in pairs." Discuss what "pair" means. Show students how to connect the cherry pairs using a black marker. Then have students make their cherry trees.

Tell each student to record the number of cherries on his or her tree at the bottom of the paper and then place the tree in the forest on the bulletin board. Have students count off the cherries by 2s: "I have 24 cherries on my tree: 2, 4, 6, 8, 10, 12, 14 … ."

Extension

Say: "What else comes in pairs?" List items students suggest, such as ears, eyes, feet, hands, and twins. Divide students into pairs. Say: "I counted 12 feet. How many children are there?" Supply students with tools such as beans and portion cups, and paper and pencils. Allow student pairs to share their strategies. Have the rest of the class ask them questions or make comments.

Say: "I counted 22 eyes. How many students are there? There is one more boy than girl. How many boys are there?"

Mismatch

Areas of Emphasis

- Mathematical Language
- Number

Group Size

- Pairs of students

Teacher Materials

- game strips master (page 19)

Student Materials

For each pair
- number cube
- game strips
- envelope
- 6 unicubes
- 6 beans

Introduction

Say: "Bidemmi's characters are always eating cherries. Let's play a game with cherries and cherry pits."

Procedure

Divide the class into pairs. Supply each pair with a number cube, game strips, an envelope, six unicubes, and six beans. (Duplicate the game strips page and cut it into strips beforehand, or have students do the cutting in their groups.)

Play the game with the class first. The pairs need to decide who will be cherries and who will be cherry pits. Choose a student to roll the number cube for the cherries. If, for example, the student rolls a 3, tell all the partners who are cherries to place 3 unicubes on their desks. Then have a student who is a cherry pit roll the number cube. If the student rolls a 6, for example, have the partners who are cherry pits get 6 beans and put 1 bean into each cube. There will be 3 beans left over. This means there are 3 more cherry pits than cherries. Tell students to put the game strip that says "3 More Cherry Pits" into the envelope. When students understand the game, have them play it with their partners. Tell them to play the game until all the game strips have been put into the envelope.

Extension

Students can play this game as an independent activity.

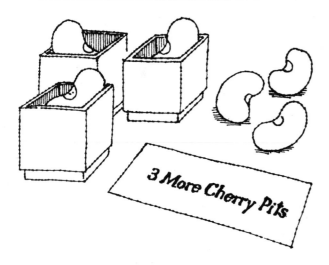

Game Strips

1 More Cherry	1 More Cherry Pit
2 More Cherries	2 More Cherry Pits
3 More Cherries	3 More Cherry Pits
4 More Cherries	4 More Cherry Pits
5 More Cherries	5 More Cherry Pits
Equal Groups	

MATH EXPLORATIONS BASED ON

Caps for Sale

by Esphyr Slobodkina

• •

A peddler who sells caps takes a nap under a tree that is filled with mischievous monkeys. He wakes from his nap to find all his caps gone. This story serves as a reminder to remain cool, calm, and collected.

Explorations	Areas of Emphasis
Monkey See, Monkey Do	Patterns Mathematical Language
More or Less	Number Mathematical Language
Cap in the Bag	Probability Statistics Mathematical Language

Monkey See, Monkey Do

Areas of Emphasis

- Patterns
- Mathematical Language

Group Size

- Whole class

Teacher Materials

- man and caps master (page 23) (optional)

Student Materials

For each student

- man and caps sheet (optional)
- crayons (optional)
- scissors (optional)
- glue (optional)

Introduction

Say: "Remember how angry the peddler became when he realized that the monkeys had taken his caps? The angrier the man became the sillier the monkeys acted. The man stamped his foot and shook his fist at the monkeys, and they stamped their feet and shook their fists at him. He got even angrier and did it again. Let's do what the man and the monkeys did: Stamp your foot, shake your fist, stamp your foot, shake your fist—a pattern. The monkeys thought they were playing a game with the man. They played it well." As you say the pattern, have the students act it out with you. "Let's see how you do with this game of patterns."

Procedure

Give your class a few more AB patterns, then move on to ABC and AAB patterns, and so on. See how long it takes students to recognize the pattern and join in.

- "Cover your eyes, cover your ears" (AB)
- "Rub your stomach, twirl around, clap" (ABC)
- "Clap, clap, hands on your head" (AAB)
- "Hop, hop, slap your knees, slap your knees" (AABB)
- "Bend your knees, jump, clap, clap" (ABCC)

Ask students how they know what will come next? Allow sufficient time for students to verbalize their understanding of the pattern.

Repeat the activity over many days, five to ten minutes at a time. Give students a chance to make up their own actions for specific patterns: AB, AAB, ABC, and so on.

Extension

This activity involves coloring and pasting caps in a pattern. Give each student a copy of the man and the caps sheet (page 23), crayons, scissors, and glue. Tell students to cut the man out and paste him on a separate piece of paper. Start the activity with an AB pattern. Say: "Color the cap on the man's head red." Continue: "Now color one of the other caps yellow." Have students color the cap, cut it out, and paste it on the man's head. Say: "Now color a cap red and paste it on the man's head." Then ask: "What color do you think the next cap will be? Why?" Have students continue on their own until they have colored and pasted all the caps. Have students discuss their work and their reasoning. This activity can be repeated with other patterns, such as ABC, AAB, and AABB.

Caps for Sale
by Esphyr Slobodkina

Man and Caps

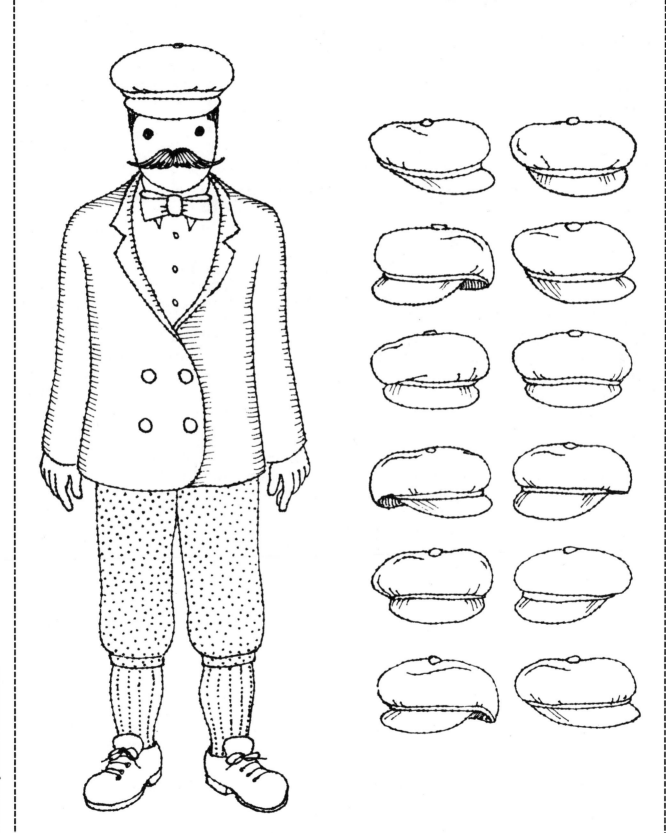

More or Less

Areas of Emphasis

- Number
- Mathematical Language

Group Size

- Pairs of students

Teacher Materials

- monkeys and caps master (page 26)

Student Materials

For each pair

- monkeys and caps sheet
- glue
- number cube (optional)
- 6 each of objects for comparison, such as pencils, crayons, and cubes (optional)

Introduction

Say: "It was a very hectic day. Sometimes the peddler would look up into the tree and there would be more monkeys, and sometimes there would be more caps. It was constantly changing. The poor man was getting confused. We are going to help him report the situation."

Procedure

Divide the class into pairs. Supply each pair with the monkeys and caps sheet. Instruct students to cut the squares out. Tell them the first scenario: "There were four monkeys in the tree. They had three caps altogether. Use your monkeys and caps to show this situation. Then match each monkey with a cap. What can you tell me about this situation?" There are two ways to describe this situation. You want students to verbalize that there is one more monkey than caps, or one less cap than monkeys.

Continue: "The man looked up into the tree again, and this time he saw three monkeys and five caps!" Again have students pair each monkey with a cap and see if they can verbalize this new situation in two ways. Keep changing the situation until you feel most of the students are working easily with the concept and the necessary language. Then let the partners create their own situations. Have them paste the monkeys and caps on a record sheet and write a description at the bottom.

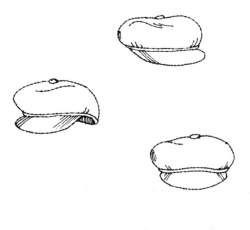

Extensions

- Say: "There are two more monkeys than caps. There are two less caps than monkeys." Instruct students to find the combinations that fit this rule. As they find the possibilities, have them glue the figures on a large sheet of butcher paper. Examples include one cap and three monkeys, two caps and four monkeys, three caps and five monkeys.

- Give each pair of students a number cube and objects (pencils, crayons, cubes, and so on). Tell one partner to roll the number cube and get that many of one type of object. Then tell the other partner to roll the number cube and gets that many of a different object. Have students describe the objects and record the comparative statements: There are four pencils. There are two crayons. There are two more pencils than crayons.

Monkeys and Caps

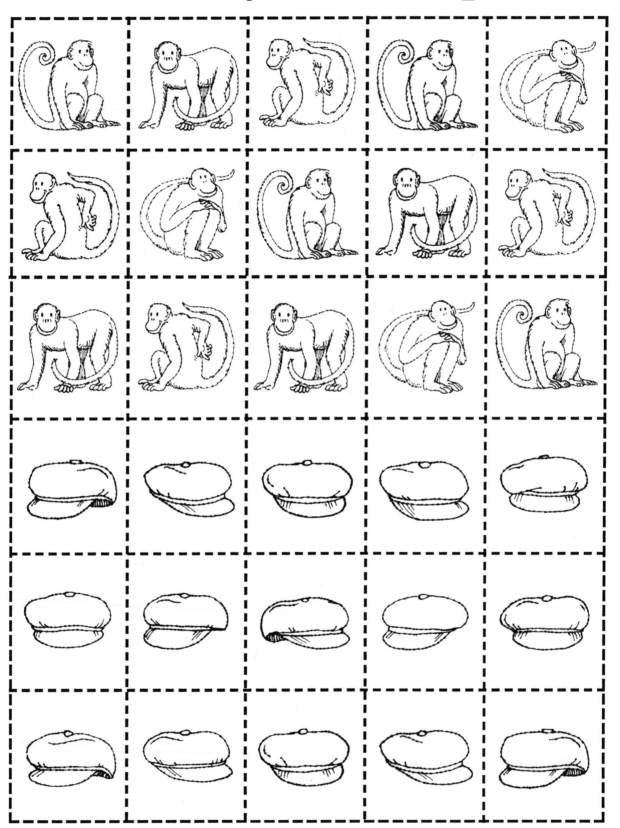

Cap in the Bag

Areas of Emphasis

- Probability
- Statistics
- Mathematical Language

Group Size

- Whole class

Teacher Materials

- caps and prediction cards master (page 29)
- paper bag
- blue crayon and red crayon
- butcher paper
- tape

Student Materials

For each student

- cap
- blue crayon and red crayon
- prediction card

Introduction

This exploration deals with using data collected from *samples* to make predictions. Students will be introduced to a variety of ways to organize this data. Then they will interpret the data and make predictions.

Before the lesson, make copies of and cut out the caps and the prediction cards. Color two of the caps blue and one red, and put these caps in a paper bag. Then give each student a paper cap, a prediction card, a blue crayon, and a red crayon. Also prepare two charts on butcher paper; one with the headings RED CAPS and BLUE CAPS (see below); and one with the headings Prediction Chart; 2 Red, 1 Blue; All Red; 2 Blue, 1 Red; All Blue (see next page). Students will sample the contents of the bag. The data will be recorded and evaluated. Then they will be asked to make a prediction based on this exploration.

Say: "I sell only red caps and blue caps. There are three caps in this bag. Do you think there are more red caps or blue caps?"

Procedure

Say:" Now we are going to sample the caps in the bag." The term *sample* is used in statistics and should be used to introduce the correct terminology. Have a student pick one cap from the bag and show the class the color. Tell the student to place the cap back in the bag and then color his or her paper cap the same color. Have the student then tape the colored cap on the recording chart under the appropriate heading.

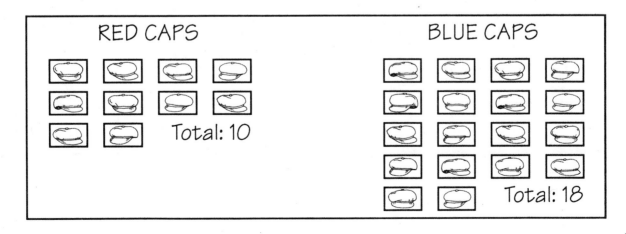

When all students have chosen a cap from the bag and taped a corresponding colored cap on the recording chart, it is time to discuss the results of the sampling. Allow enough time for the class to share. Then give each student a prediction card. Have students color the caps on the card according to their prediction of what color caps are in the bag: 2 red, 1 blue; all red; 2 blue, 1 red; or all blue. When they bring up their cards, ask them why they are making this particular prediction. Tape the cards in columns on the prediction chart for easy comparison. Show the contents of the bag and discuss the results. Repeat the activity with a different combination of colors another day.

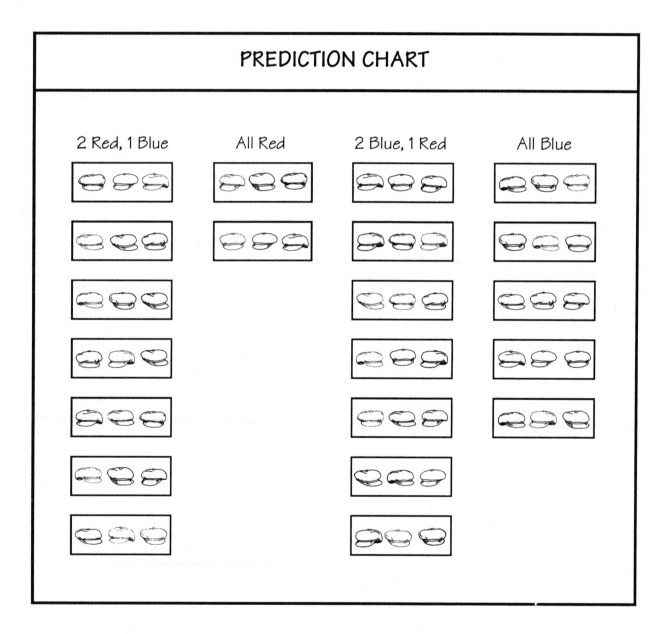

PREDICTION CHART

2 Red, 1 Blue   All Red   2 Blue, 1 Red   All Blue

Caps

   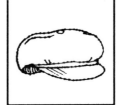 

Prediction Cards

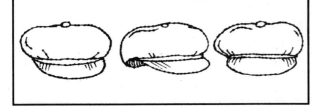 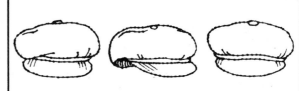

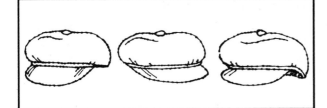 

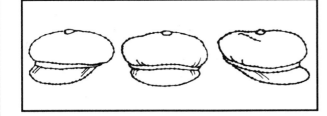 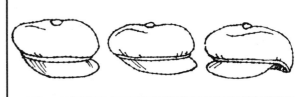

MATH EXPLORATIONS BASED ON

Corduroy

by Don Freeman

• •

Corduroy, a stuffed bear who lives in the toy department of a big store, waits for a child to come along and take him home. He's missing a button on his overalls, so he searches all over the store for one—without success. But a little girl named Lisa buys him anyway, sews a button on his overalls, and becomes his friend.

Explorations	Areas of Emphasis
My Favorite Button	Logic: attributes Mathematical Language
Small, Medium, Big	Measurement Mathematical Language Number
What's My Rule?	Logic: attributes Mathematical Language
Button Factory	Number: place value, writing numbers Measurement Estimation Mathematical Language

My Favorite Button

Areas of Emphasis

- Logic: attributes
- Mathematical Language

Group Size

- 3–5 students

Student Materials

For each group

- small plastic bag of 6–10 different buttons
- self-lock bags or envelopes (1 per student)
- glue

Introduction

Say: "Pretend that you are Corduroy and want to look your best. Choose a special button for your jacket." Remind students to be thinking about why they chose a particular button.

Procedure

Divide the class into small groups. Give each group a bag of buttons. This is the easiest part for you—just mingle and listen as students discuss the problem. Remind students to look carefully at the buttons to identify similarities and differences.

Have each student store his or her button in an envelope or self-lock bag. Say: "This is your favorite button. If you lost this button, you would want to get it back. You would have to describe it so people would recognize your button if they found it. Tell me something about your button." Model descriptive language for the class. Show them your favorite button. List different characteristics of your button: "My button is red, round, and has two holes. It is small and shiny." Let everyone share. Then have students record the attributes of their button on a sheet of paper. Tell them to use best-guess spelling at this point. Let them glue their button on the description sheet.

Extension

Let each student share his or her button and its characteristics from the description sheet. Students, even the nonreaders, will remember their descriptive words. They are reading!

Natalie's button

1. My button has to holes
2. My button is a curcil
3. My button has Defret colors: red yellow pink blue purpel black
4. My button is smal

Corduroy
by Don Freeman

• •

Small, Medium, Big

Areas of Emphasis

- Measurement
- Mathematical Language
- Number

Group Size

- Individuals in small groups

Teacher Materials

- an assortment of buttons

Student Materials

For each group

- a bank of buttons (about 20 buttons per student)
- calculator (optional)

Introduction

Show the class a button. Ask students how they would describe the size of the button. Have students share their opinions on the size only. Now choose a button that is smaller than the first button. Show both of the buttons. Ask: "How would you now describe the size of the original button?" Show a third button. This should be bigger than the original button. Ask: "How would you now describe the size of the original button? What happened? Why did our descriptions of the original button change?" This is an opportunity for substantial language development.

Procedure

This is a lesson for individuals in small groups for easy management and language interaction. Give each group a bank of buttons. Direct each student to take 10 buttons at random. Tell students not to pick buttons that follow a rule (for example, all red or all four-hole). You may want to model this first step. Instruct students to line up the buttons from smallest to largest. After they have done this, let some students share their strategies for determining relative size: "I put the buttons on top of each other, and then I could see which one was bigger."

Then have students decide which buttons are small, medium, and big. Model this for students: Divide the buttons into three piles according to size. Place each pile on a piece of paper. Draw a circle around each pile. Count the buttons in each pile and write that number in the circle. Model the number sentence for your button group: "I have 4 small buttons and 3 medium buttons and 3 big buttons. That makes 10 buttons in all." Tell students that you are making a record of this investigation. Say: "Mathematicians should always record the results of an investigation." You may want to let them check their number sentence with a calculator. Repeat this activity with 10 buttons a few more times. Try 11 buttons another day. Always adjust the lesson goals to meet the individual needs of your class.

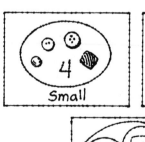

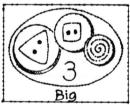

$4 + 3 + 3 = 10$ Buttons

What's My Rule?

Areas of Emphasis

- Logic: attributes
- Mathematical Language

Group Size

- 3–5 students

Teacher Materials

- small plastic bag of 6–7 buttons that share an attribute
- marker
- assortment of objects (optional)

Student Materials

For each student

- small plastic bag of 6–7 buttons that share an attribute

Introduction

Prepare a small plastic bag of buttons for each group. Each bag should contain 6–7 buttons that share an attribute (for example, 4-hole buttons, large buttons, or green buttons). Number the bags with a marker.

Tell the class that you have gone through your button collection and have put certain buttons together in bags. Each bag of buttons follows a different rule. Their job will be to figure out the rule.

Procedure

Divide the class into groups of 3–5 students. Give each group a sheet of paper to record their findings. Examine a bag of buttons first with the entire class. Bring out one button at a time. Ask students to tell you everything about this button (size, color, shape, number of holes, and so on). Remember, you are the facilitator. Only ask questions; do not give the answers. List the attributes of each button on the chalkboard. After students have discussed the attributes, ask if there is a rule that all the buttons in the bag follow. Allow time for students to listen to each other and weigh the possibilities. Record on the chalkboard the rule that they decide on; for example: All the buttons in the bag have two holes.

Tell the groups that they are now ready to be detectives. Remind them that mathematicians record their findings. They may choose one person in the group to record the attributes of each button on a recording sheet, or they may take turns. Circulate and provide assistance as needed. Remind students to write a rule that applies to all the buttons in their bag. Tell them that it is possible that their bag of buttons will have more than one rule. Allow 10–15 minutes for this part of the activity.

Review the recording sheets with the entire class. Some groups might come up with an unusual rule. If all the buttons in the bag follow that rule, then the rule is valid! Write the number of each bag on the chalkboard and record the bag's rule or rules.

Extension

Show the class an assortment of other objects, such as a wooden ruler, some wooden beads, a pencil, plastic foam peanuts, a tennis shoe, a book, and a spring from a broken toy. Say: "See if you can group some of these objects and come up with a rule for them." Some of the rules that my students made up were: "things that are wood" and "things that are shaped like a rectangle." It was interesting to hear the groups present their rules. The class was amazed at the number of valid rules that applied to the groups of objects.

Button Factory

Areas of Emphasis

- Number: place value, writing numbers
- Measurement
- Estimation
- Mathematical Language

Group Size

- 4–6 students

Teacher Materials

- large sheet of butcher paper
- watch with a second hand

Student Materials

For each student

- container of about 40 pennies (optional)
- nickels and dimes (optional)

Introduction

Say to students: "Buttons, buttons, buttons! We've been doing a lot of investigations with buttons. I'm going to put you to work today to see how many buttons you can make."

Procedure

This is an individual lesson that will be managed in small groups of 4–6 students. Distribute paper and have students draw a square in a corner of their paper. Tell them to divide this box into two triangles by connecting two opposite corners. Demonstrate the procedure on a large sheet of butcher paper. Tell students that this is their "Guess Box." The top triangle is for their estimate, and the bottom triangle is for the actual count.

Say: "I am going to give you one minute to draw buttons. How many buttons do you think you can make in one minute? Remember, buttons have holes!" Let students discuss this question with the members of their group before recording their estimates in the Guess Box. After everyone, including you, has written an estimate, start the timed minute. While students are working, model the activity on the butcher paper.

When the minute is up, draw students' attention to your sheet of buttons. Circle groups of ten buttons. "I made two groups of ten and six single buttons." Write the total number of buttons you made in the bottom triangle of the Guess Box.

Tell students to circle groups of ten buttons on their sheet and then record the total number of buttons in the lower part of the Guess Box. Encourage them to check each other's work. Stress the language of writing their numbers: "How many tens did you make? How many single buttons were left?" Let students share how many buttons they made and how their actual number compared with their estimate. Repeat the activity a few more times. Students' estimates should get closer to the actual counts.

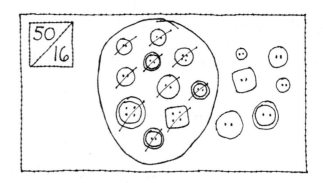

Extension

Give each student a container of pennies, and say: "It's payday! You will get a penny for each button you made." Tell students to place a penny on each button they drew and then count the number of coins. Everyone's amount must be checked by at least one other member of the group. Then let students exchange every five pennies for a nickel. Have them record the amount on their paper. At the end of the activity, have students return the coins to you.

You can vary this activity by having students place a nickel on each button in a group of ten and a penny on the singles. Or, the buttons that have two holes can be worth a nickel, and the buttons that have four holes can be worth a dime.

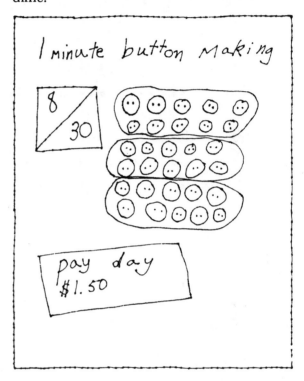

MATH EXPLORATIONS BASED ON

The Doorbell Rang

by Pat Hutchins

Ma has made a dozen cookies for Victoria and Sam to share. Each time the doorbell rings, more friends are welcomed in to share the cookies. More and more children mean fewer and fewer cookies to go around.

Explorations	Areas of Emphasis
From the Ground Up	Statistics: graphing Number Mathematical Language
Dozens of Cookies	Number Statistics Mathematical Language
Exploring with a Dozen	Patterns Geometry Number Problem Solving Mathematical Language
Friends Share	Number: beginning division Statistics Mathematical Language

From the Ground Up

Areas of Emphasis

- Statistics: graphing
- Number
- Mathematical Language

Group Size

- 3–4 students

Teacher Materials

- large sheet of butcher paper

Student Materials

For each student
- 2" x 2" piece of paper

Introduction

Remind students that *The Doorbell Rang* is about some children sharing and eating the best cookies ever! Ask students if they have a favorite cookie. Record the information on a language experience chart or on the chalkboard.

My Favorite Cookie

Carla likes oatmeal raisin cookies best.
Daniel likes chocolate chip cookies best.
Cameron likes gingersnaps best.
Rachel likes chocolate chip cookies best.

Procedure

Divide the class into groups of 3–4 students. Ask them to use the language experience chart to find out how many children liked chocolate chip cookies the best. Suggest that they have some members of the group read the chart and others tally the information. The exercise will take them a considerable amount of time. Bring the class together when groups are finished, and have students discuss the results of their research. Encourage students to share the difficulties they encountered in using the language experience chart to obtain the answer.

chocolate chip
+++++ ///

Keep the class together for this next step. Say: "I have some more questions for you to answer based on the 'favorite cookie' information. It will be very time consuming for you if the information is kept on the chart. We can organize the favorite cookie information in a way that will be much easier for you to use. We can record this information in a mathematical way. It is called graphing. The graph we will make today is called a bar graph."

Give each student a square of paper approximately 2" x 2". Tell students to write the name of their favorite cookie on the square and draw a picture of it. Now tape a large piece of butcher paper on a wall or the chalkboard. Draw a base line across the bottom of the paper. Tell the class that this is where each cookie tower will start. Explain to them that a graph is built like a house—from the ground up! Have students come up one at a time and tell what their favorite cookie is and then tape the square on the graph. A new tower is started whenever a new cookie is introduced. Write the name of the cookie below each tower.

After everyone has placed his or her square on the graph, draw the vertical lines and then the horizontal lines. Point to the rows as you explain the procedure. Say: "This is where there is one cookie in each tower, so I will write a 1 on the far left of my graph. This is where there are two cookies in each tower, so I will write a 2 on the far left of my graph."

Ask students questions such as the following: "How many children like chocolate chip cookies best? How many children like chocolate

37

chip cookies more than oatmeal cookies? What is the least favorite cookie?" Ask some higher-level thinking questions: "Why do you think more children like chocolate chip cookies best? Do you think we would get the same graph from another group of second graders? What do you think a favorite-cookie graph would look like if we asked adults about their favorite cookies?"

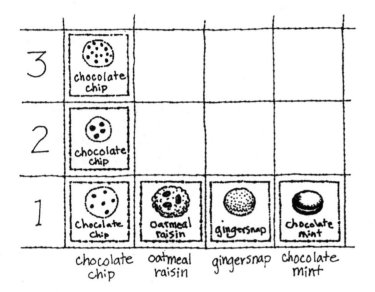

Dozens of Cookies

Areas of Emphasis

- Number
- Statistics
- Mathematical Language

Group Size

- 3–4 students

Student Materials

For each group

- a bank of at least 60 counters
- calculator (optional)

Introduction

Ask: "How many cookies are in a dozen?" Have students display a dozen counters.

Procedure

Divide the class into groups of 3–4 students. Say: "We are going to explore with dozens. I will record what we find out on a T-Table. You will make a T-Table, too." Explain to students that tables organize facts. Tables have headings; a T-Table has two headings. Using a table makes it easier to see whether a pattern exists.

Dozen	Cookies
1	12

Continue: "How many cookies are in two dozen? How can you find out to be sure?" Wait until all the groups have displayed two groups of 12 counters. Record the numbers on the table. Repeat with three, four, and five dozen. Use exact oral language as you make the entries on the table: "There are 12 cookies in one dozen. There are 24 cookies in two dozen." Direct students to look at the patterns that are developing on both sides of the table. "Do you see any patterns on either side of the table?" Possible responses: "The left side of the table has a counting-by-ones pattern." "The right column has a counting-by-twos pattern in the single digits of the numbers."

Dozen	Cookies
1	12
2	24
3	36
4	48
5	60

Ask: "How many cookies are in ten dozen?" Let students use calculators if they wish. Also encourage them to look for number patterns on the table. When I did this with a group of second graders, they found many patterns on the table: "I can check if I'm right by doubling the number. 1 and 1 is 2 and there is a 2 in 12,; 2 and 2 makes 4 and there is a 4 in 24." Another student noticed a different pattern: "I see a 2, 4, 6, 8, 10 pattern on the right side."

Extension

Say: "We will make four dozen cookies. Everyone in the class will get one cookie. How many cookies will we have left over?" Tell students they may use any mathematical tools they wish. They must record their work and be prepared to present their strategies to the class.

Facts
(23 kids)

4 dozen
↓
48

$48 - 23 = 25$

We will have 25 extra cookies

(tool: cubes)

Exploring with a Dozen

Areas of Emphasis

- Patterns
- Geometry
- Number
- Problem Solving
- Mathematical Language

Group Size

- 3–5 students

Student Materials

For each group

- manipulatives (one type per station): tiles, beans, beads, cubes
- graph paper (Tile Station)
- portion cups (Cups and Beans Station)
- paper clips (Cups and Beans Station)

Introduction

Set up stations around the classroom. Provide materials for manipulation and recording. Display directions for each station as shown below. Ask: "What can you make with a dozen? Let's find out today."

Procedure

Divide the class into groups of 3–5 students. Assign each group to a station. Tell the groups that they will choose a dozen of the material that is at their station. Each station will have a project for them. They will have approximately twenty minutes to complete the exploration and record their findings.

Tile Station

Get a dozen tiles. Make a rectangle with the tiles. Record the rectangle on graph paper. How many different rectangles can you make? Record each one.

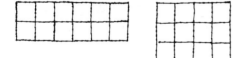

Cups and Beans Station

Join three portion cups with paper clips. Get a dozen beans. Divide them among the three cups. Record the results in a number sentence. How many different ways can you divide the beans? Write a number sentence for each one.

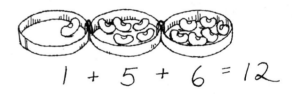

$$1 + 5 + 6 = 12$$

Beads Station

Look at the beads. Discuss their color, size, and shape. Think about an AB pattern. Choose a dozen beads. Make a necklace that has an AB pattern. Record your design.

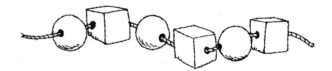

Cubes Station

Get a dozen cubes. Build a house with different levels and rooms. All the cubes must touch at least one cube. Draw a picture of your house.

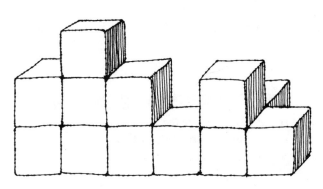

Extension

Let students use two dozen items for an independent exploration. This activity can be set up as an individual or partner exploration. Students may share their creations with the rest of the class instead of making a record.

Friends Share

Areas of Emphasis

- Number: beginning division
- Statistics
- Mathematical Language

Group Size

- 4–6 students

Student Materials

For each group

- 12 paper plates
- 12 cookies or paper cookies
- ingredients and equipment for baking cookies (optional)

Safety Note

If you wish to allow students to eat the cookies after the activity, be sure to obtain parents' or guardians' permission beforehand in case of allergies or other dietary restrictions.

Introduction

Tell the class that you are going to read *The Doorbell Rang* to them and then they will experience what the characters in the book experience.

Procedure

Divide the class into groups of 4–6 students. Supply each group with a dozen paper plates and a dozen cookies. Say: "Every cookie eater in the story must have a plate." Start the story and have each group put out two plates—one for Sam and one for Victoria. Ma tells Sam and Victoria to share the cookies. "How many cookies will each of them get?" Record the sharing results on a table.

Sharing Table

People	Cookies
2	6 each
4	3 each
6	2 each
12	1 each

Continue reading to where Tom and Hannah arrive. "How many children are there now? Yes, there are four; Tom and Hannah will get some cookies, too." Tell students to put out a plate for Tom and a plate for Hannah. Ask them to predict how many cookies each child will get. After they have shared their ideas, tell them to divide the cookies among the four plates. Record the information on the table.

Continue reading the story. Each time the doorbell rings and more children come in, ask the groups to predict the number of cookies each child will get. Then have them divide the cookies on the plates and give reasons for their ideas. You want them to become comfortable articulating their thinking and strategies. Continue to record the information on the table.

Extension

Organize a cooking center and have each group of students make cookies. Have each group follow the same recipe. Groups should record how many cookies they were able to make from the recipe and how many cookies they each got. When all groups have made cookies bring the class together and discuss the sharing.

MATH EXPLORATIONS BASED ON

Mr. Gumpy's Outing

by John Burningham

• •

Mr. Gumpy lives by the river and owns a boat. He takes his friends out on his boat. They try to be polite, but when you invite a goat, a calf, some chickens, sheep, a pig, a dog, a cat, a rabbit, and two children, there are bound to be some mishaps.

Explorations	Areas of Emphasis
Signs for Travel	Mathematical Language: connecting mathematical symbols to language
How Many Travelers?	Number Mathematical Language: connecting mathematical symbols to language
Who's in the Boat?	Number Logic Measurement Mathematical Language
Possibilities	Logic Problem Solving Mathematical Language
Leftover Baggage	Number Logic Mathematical Language
Heads and Legs	Problem Solving Number Mathematical Language

Signs for Travel

Area of Emphasis

■ Mathematical Language:
  connecting mathematical symbols to
  language

Group Size

■ 4–6 students

Student Materials

For each group

■ paper
■ crayons

Introduction

This exploration deals with the important beginnings of relating the oral language of mathematics to the symbolic language of mathematics. Too often this crucial step is forgotten or gone over too quickly. The first step is to show why and how symbolic language is created. The character of Mr. Gumpy is used to make this connection.

Say: "Last week Mr. Gumpy had laryngitis and couldn't speak. He still wanted to take the boat out every day. He came up with the brilliant idea of making signs that would communicate for him! If he was going north on the river, he used a sign that showed a picture of the town on it. If he was going south on the river, he showed a sign that had a picture of the ocean on it. What do you think the picture of an empty boat meant?" Record responses on the chalkboard. Say: "Everyone on the river loved this new way of communicating. The children, the animals, and the townspeople started to make signs for everything they wanted to say!"

Procedure

Ask students to think of types of picture signs they see or use in their daily lives (for example, road signs, weather symbols, travel signs, medical alert/poison signs). List their responses on the chalkboard. (You may wish to invite students to draw pictures of the signs as an independent activity.) Discuss instances in which picture signs may be more appropriate than written messages. Some of the points that should come out of this discussion include overcoming language barriers, reaching nonreaders, and providing immediate communication for emergency situations.

Next, have the class suggest parts of the school day that would need a picture sign if verbal communication were impossible. These might include silent reading time, lunch time, recess, math time, and getting into cooperative groups. Divide the class into groups of 4–6 students. Assign signs to each group. Students should discuss the design possibilities and work together to create the picture signs.

Extension

Have a day of minimal verbal communication, and use the signs students created.

How Many Travelers?

Areas of Emphasis

- Number
- Mathematical Language: connecting mathematical symbols to language

Group Size

- Pairs of students

Teacher Materials

- Mr. Gumpy's boat master (page 47)
- bank of animals master (page 48)
- + and − cards (optional)

Student Materials

For each pair

- Mr. Gumpy's boat sheet
- bank of animals sheet
- scissors
- counters (optional)

Introduction

In this exploration, students make an initial connection from the oral language to the symbolic language of math. Say: "Today we are going to go along with Mr. Gumpy on his trips up and down the river." Note: This exploration must be preceded by "Signs for Travel" (page 44).

Procedure

Divide the class into pairs of students. Supply each pair with a picture of Mr. Gumpy's boat and a bank of animals. Have them cut out the animal squares. Tell students to listen to the instructions and follow the signs Mr. Gumpy gives. Write "Trip 1" on the chalkboard and say: "Mr. Gumpy went down to the big bend in the river and picked up three animals." As you say this, write the symbolic language +3 under Trip 1. Let each pair of students decide which three animals go in the boat. Ask the pairs to share their combinations. Continue: "Mr. Gumpy stopped at the bend in the river and let one more animal on." As you say this, write on the chalkboard +1. Make a quick assessment of the class; notice which pairs are discussing what they should do and choosing an animal from their bank. Ask: "How many travelers are in the boat now?" (4) "What happened? Can someone tell me?" Allow time for discussion, language development, and sharing of ideas.

Now tell the class: "The wind really picked up and the river was getting rough. Some of the animals started to get sick, and two of them got off the boat at the next stop." As you tell them this, write −2 on the chalkboard. Tell students that this is the way a mathematician would write what happened. Say: "How many animals are in the boat now?" (2) Allowing adequate time for discussion in a nonjudgmental atmosphere will promote your students' mathematical language. Questions that encourage students to think and explain their thinking help them to understand the concepts.

Continue with the story: "The little boat finally made it to the town. No one got off the boat. There were three animals that needed a ride back up the river, and they got on the boat quickly." Write +3 on the chalkboard as you give students this information. Ask: "How many animals are in the boat now?" (5) Allow time to share responses.

Continue the story: "At the big bend in the river, four animals got off the boat since it was almost lunch time and they were expected at home." Write −4 on the chalkboard as you give them this information. Ask: "How many animals are in the boat now?" (1) Continue: "Mr. Gumpy let one more animal off the boat at the big oak tree just before his pier." Write −1 on the chalkboard. "How many are left in Mr. Gumpy's boat now?" (0)

In the second part of this lesson, students use symbolic instructions alone to change the number of animals in their boat. Tell them that they are going on another trip with Mr. Gumpy and some of the animals. This time you will tell how many animals got on and off the boat without ever saying a word! Ask if anyone knows how you will be able to do this. Someone might remind you about the numbers and the signs that you used during the first boat ride. If no one volunteers this information, remind students that in mathematics the sign used to take something away looks like this: −, and the sign used to add something looks like this: +. The number that follows these signs tells you how many to either take away or add. Give a few examples: −1, +4, +2, −3. Each time, give the oral language that goes with each symbolic instruction. When most of the students understand, proceed with Trip 2. Remind the pairs that they must discuss each move before touching the animals. They may choose any animals for the trip but they must obey the signs. Keep the initial number under 5. Start out with +3, and watch to see whether the pairs discuss and then choose the appropriate number of animals for their boat. Limit this first symbolic trip to four or five instructions to keep the attention level high.

At the end of the trip, ask students how many animals they have in their boats. This is a good time to develop language of combinations: "We have one cow and one pig; that makes two animals." If the class's interest level is still high, it would be appropriate to do another trip. If not, this activity should be repeated at another time. One trip per day would give concrete experience with the mathematical symbols.

Extension

Make + and − cards to do quick exercises with the class. Each student will need a bank of counters. Hold up a card: +3. When everyone has three counters displayed, hold up another card: −1. Limit the number of instruction cards to four or five in the beginning. You might see a lot of confusion when you throw in a −0 or +0 card, but this is a great time for the students to learn about zeros.

Use with "How Many Travelers?,"
"Who's in the Boat?," and "Heads and Legs."

Mr. Gumpy's Outing
by John Burningham

Mr. Gumpy's Boat

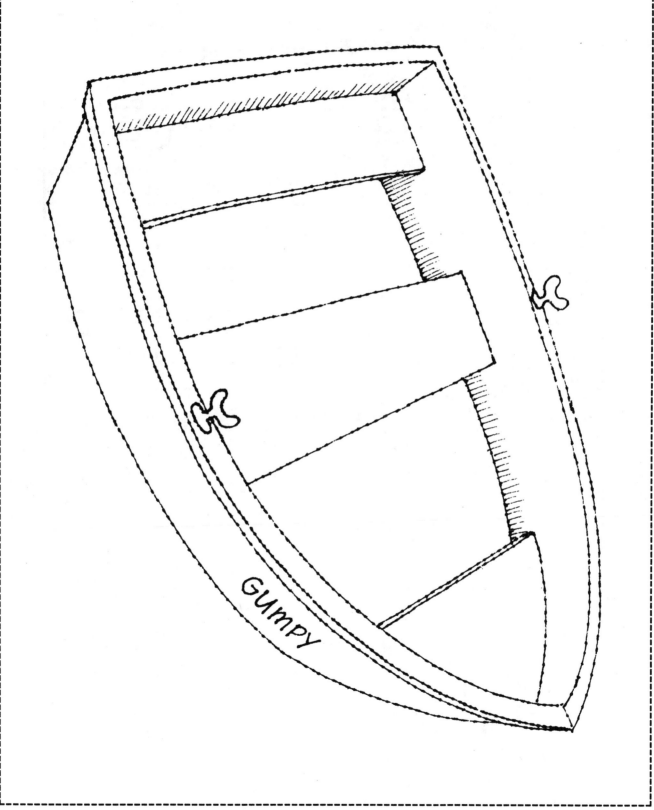

Bank of Animals

Who's in the Boat?

Areas of Emphasis

- Number
- Logic
- Measurement
- Mathematical Language

Group Size

- Pairs of students

Teacher Materials

- Mr. Gumpy's boat master (page 47)
- bank of animals master (page 48)

Student Materials

For each pair

- Mr. Gumpy's boat sheet
- bank of animals sheet
- scissors

Introduction

Say: "Every morning Mr. Gumpy goes to the bank of the river and takes some animals for a ride. Mr. Gumpy gives them clues so that they can figure out who will be included on the ride that day."

Procedure

Divide the class into pairs of students. Supply each pair with a boat and a bank of animals. Have them cut out the animal squares. As you give students the clues, write them on the chalkboard so that you can review them as you go along. At first the students might react to each clue separately without using the preceding clues. Repeat the clues in the order that you gave them.

RIDE 1

First clue: "It's a beautiful Sunday morning, and Mr. Gumpy gets to the bank of the river just as the sun is coming up. There are pigs, dogs, cats, and rabbits waiting patiently. Mr. Gumpy says, 'There can be only three animals in my boat today.'" Tell the class that this is the first clue. They should discuss with their partners what the possibilities are and agree on a combination before they actually place the animals in the boat. As you go around the room, ask each pair what their combination is: "My partner and I have two pigs and one dog." "Beth and I have one pig and one cat and one rabbit." This oral sharing is very important in the students' math development.

Second clue: "Mr. Gumpy then tells them that there can't be any dogs or rabbits in the boat today." Again make sure that the partners discuss the clue before they start making any changes in their boats. Ask some of the pairs to share what animals they now have in their boats. "My partner and I have two cats and one pig." "Carlos and I have three cats." If a pair hasn't used the clues to come up with a logical decision, direct them to the clues again.

Third clue: "There are more pigs than cats."

Discuss the process of finding what the combination really is. Allow pairs time to share their thoughts. After each boat ride, you will see students getting better at listening to the clues and discussing the possibilities. This lesson is a great way to introduce new mathematical language and concepts. As students get better, you can increase the skill/concept level to accommodate their progress.

RIDE 2

"There are five animals in the boat."
"There are only dogs and cats in the boat."
"There are more cats than dogs."
"There is one more cat than there are dogs."

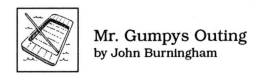

● ●

RIDE 3

"There are more than three and less than five animals in the boat."

"Half of the animals in the boat are rabbits."

"There is an equal number of pigs and rabbits."

RIDE 4

"There are less than eight and more than five animals in the boat."

"There is an even number of animals in the boat."

"Half of the animals are cats."

"There is an equal number of cats and pigs."

RIDE 5

"There are as many animals as there are days in a week."

"There are only rabbits and pigs in the boat."

"There is an odd number of pigs in the boat."

"There are less than three pigs in the boat."

Possibilities

Areas of Emphasis

- Logic
- Problem Solving
- Mathematical Language

Group Size

- Pairs of students

Teacher Materials

- cat, dog, and pig master (page 52)
- recording sheet master (page 53)

Student Materials

For each pair
- cat, dog, and pig sheet
- scissors
- paste
- recording sheet

Introduction

Problem solving involves students sharing their ideas, planning strategies, and evaluating the results. It also means developing an appreciation for the process of solving problems as well as finding solutions. The following exploration fosters this type of emphasis. Say: "Mr. Gumpy is having a problem with the cat, dog, and pig. They always travel together, and they always argue. They all want to sit in the front of the boat. Mr. Gumpy is tired of their constant squabbling. Let's help him find a solution to this problem. Does anyone have any suggestions?"

Procedure

Direct your questioning toward the realization that the cat, dog, and pig must take turns in all the possible seating arrangements. Divide the class into pairs. Supply each pair with the animals, scissors, paste, and the recording sheet. Tell students to find a possible seating arrangement and paste the animals in that order in a boat on the recording sheet.

When the class has recorded the first seating arrangement, instruct pairs to find a different seating arrangement. Assist as necessary. "Has each animal had a chance to ride in the middle seat? Has each animal had a chance to ride in the back seat?" Remind students to check carefully the originality of a new seating arrangement before pasting it on the recording sheet. There are six possible seating arrangements: cat-dog-pig, cat-pig-dog, pig-cat-dog, pig-dog-cat, dog-pig-cat, and dog-cat-pig.

Bring the class together to share their findings. How long you give pairs to explore this situation is up to you. As you walk around observing and assessing, you will know who has been successful and who is becoming frustrated.

Extension

You may wish to give the class three new animals: calf, rabbit, and goat (see page 48). Tell the pairs to find and record all the possible seating arrangements for these animals.

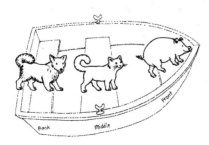

Cat, Dog, and Pig

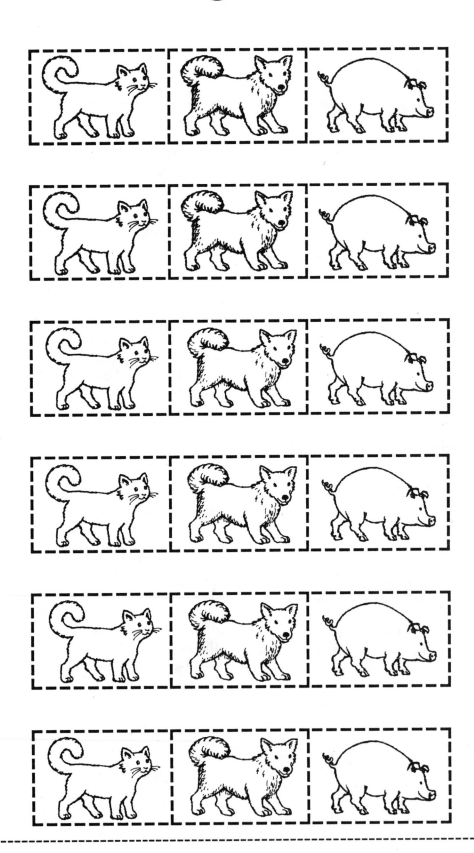

Recording Sheet

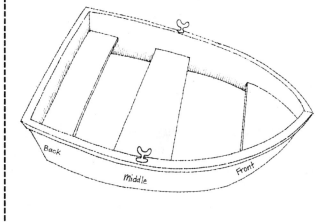

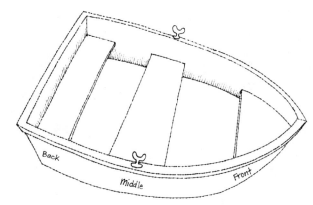

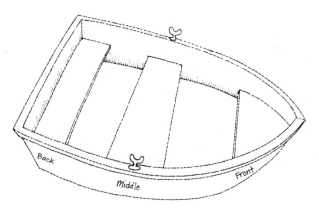

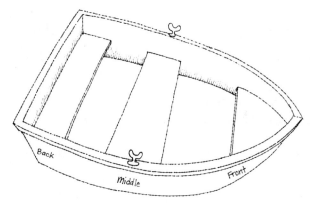

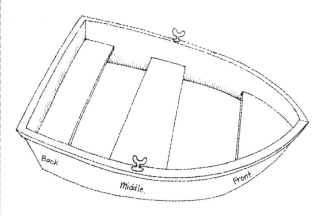

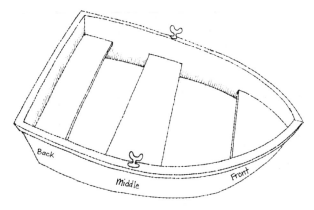

Names _____

Leftover Baggage

Areas of Emphasis

- Number
- Logic
- Mathematical Language

Group Size

- Whole class

Teacher Materials

- note to Mr. Gumpy
- paper bag
- 17 beans

Student Materials

For each pair

- 100 charts (optional)
- Unifix® cubes (optional)
- scissors (optional)

Introduction

Before the exploration begins, copy the following note to Mr. Gumpy on a piece of paper. Fold the paper and, on the front, write "Mr. Gumpy." Put 17 beans into a bag and attach the note to the bag. This exploration will captivate your students the minute they see the bag with the note addressed to Mr. Gumpy attached. I tell students that Mr. Gumpy found the bag in his boat at the end of the day. The bag has a mystery to be solved. Then read the note to the class:

> Dear Mr. Gumpy,
> Here are the beans you ordered for your garden. You told me to give you more than 3 and less than 20. I hope I've sent you the correct amount. Your garden always looks so nice.
>
> From your friend,
> Otto—at the feed store.

Procedure

Write a number line (1–25) on the chalkboard or butcher paper. Ask: "What number of beans cannot be in this bag?" Be sure students give reasons for their responses. If they are correct, cross that number off the number line. Praise good mathematical language. "You're right! There cannot be two beans in the bag because that is not more than three. It is less than three." Continue until you have eliminated the numbers that do not follow the rule: more than 3 and less than 20.

X̶ X̶ X̶ 4 5 6 7 8 9 10 11 12 13 14 15 16 17 18 19 X̶ X̶ X̶ X̶ X̶ X̶ X̶

Tell students that Otto told you how many beans are in the bag. Let students guess what the number is. For example, if a student guesses 12, you respond: "The number of beans in the bag is more than 12." Now ask the class what numbers can be eliminated. As they give them, cross them off the number line. Continue in this way until the class finds the number.

Repeat the activity. This time make the number line from 1–30. Write down the secret number on a piece of paper so that you don't forget it in the middle of the activity. This will also model the appropriate procedure for when the students play in small groups. Continue, using the same format. Repeat the game with a longer number line if your class is ready.

Extension

Let students continue with this activity in pairs. I give each pair a 100 chart to cut up and glue together in a horizontal line, using as many groups of ten as needed for the number line. It is easier for them to follow the sequence of the numbers this way. They can put a cube on the numbers that have been disqualified. Partners can take turns choosing the secret number. They should use tally marks to keep track of the number of guesses made. The goal should be to find the number as fast as they can. Make sure that the number that is chosen is written down to avoid the possibility of middle-of-the-game changes. After the class has played, ask: "What is your strategy for finding the answer quickly?"

Heads and Legs

Areas of Emphasis

- Problem Solving
- Number
- Mathematical Language

Group Size

- Individuals

Teacher Materials

- Mr. Gumpy's boat master (page 47)
- cows and ducks master (page 58)

Student Materials

For each student

- Mr. Gumpy's boat sheet
- cows and ducks sheet

Introduction

"Mr. Gumpy likes to give his duck and cow friends a ride in his boat. He also likes to give children riddles. I am going to show you a way to solve his Heads and Legs riddles." Give each student a boat and some cows and ducks. Tell students to cut out the animal squares and put three animals in their boat. Tell them they must include at least one duck and one cow.

Ask: "How many legs are in your boat? How many heads are in your boat?" Help students determine the number of possible combinations of animals (two combinations: 1 duck, 2 cows; 2 ducks, 1 cow). Then have them count the heads and legs in each combination. Record the information on the chalkboard. Repeat the activity until you feel students are comfortable with the format of recording.

1 Duck, 2 Cows	2 Ducks, 1 Cow
3 heads	3 heads
10 legs	8 legs

Procedure

Now the class is ready for the first riddle. "Mr. Gumpy decided to take only ducks and cows on his boat this morning. He took a total of four animals. He told me he counted ten legs. He wants us to find out who was in his boat. I know that there were at least one duck and one cow aboard." Begin a class discussion of the facts of this situation. List the information students give: There are four animals in the boat, so there are four heads; there is at least one duck; there is at least one cow; a cow has four legs; a duck has two legs.

Move around the room and assist students who are struggling. You will find you need to remind them that Mr. Gumpy said there were only four animals in the boat. Encourage them to figure all the possible combinations of animals and then count the number of legs.

1 Duck, 3 Cows	2 Ducks, 2 Cows	3 Ducks, 1 Cow
4 heads	4 heads	4 heads
14 legs	12 legs	10 legs

Encourage students to keep trying if their first combination did not prove to be correct. No one expects them to get it the first time. You want to emphasize persistence, not speed. If someone has found the answer, tell him or her to wait and share when everyone has finished.

When everyone has solved the riddle and shared his or her strategy, introduce recording the results with a picture. Show them how to draw stick figures of a cow and a duck. Some children get stressed out because they feel they cannot draw, and some spend the entire work period drawing. Suggest that they use a pencil instead of crayons.

4 animals. 10 Legs.
4 Heads

Cynthia

Extension

Let the students make up their own "Heads and Legs" riddles. Remember to give them sufficient experience before you ask them to create their own riddles. Encourage them to share their riddles with classmates.

Praise the persistence students demonstrate. They are ready for another challenge. This can be given the same day or another day. "Mr. Gumpy had 4 animals in his boat the next day, still only cows and ducks. This time he counted 12 legs." Repeat the same procedure. During the investigation, you will notice that some students have gained a lot from the previous investigation. Always allow enough time to share; they learn so much from each other. Continue with 4 animals and 14 legs, or make up a new boat problem.

Cows and Ducks

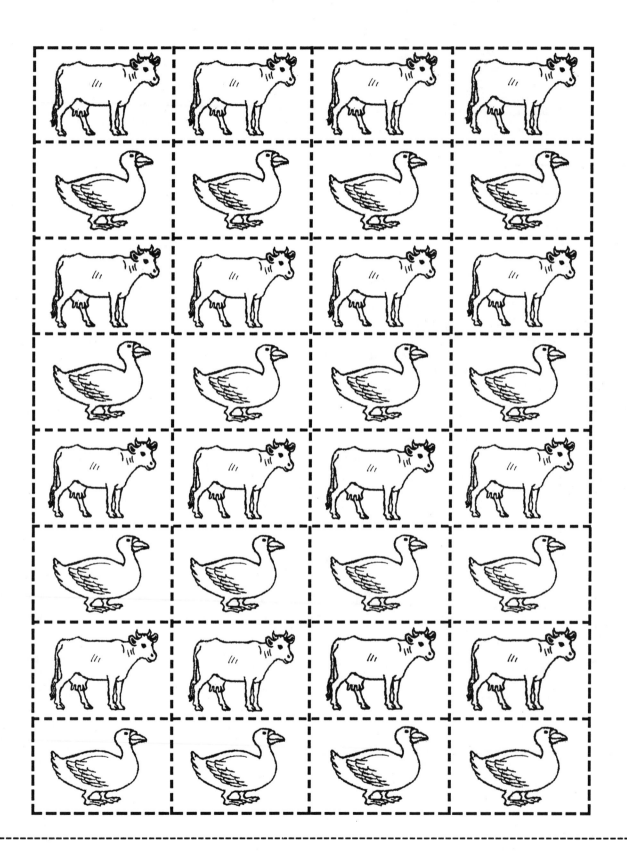

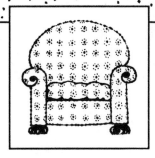

MATH EXPLORATIONS BASED ON

A Chair for My Mother

by Vera B. Williams

When a fire destroys everything, a family needs to replace a big, comfortable chair. Little by little, everyone deposits spare change into a large glass jar until there's enough money to buy a new chair. This is a wonderful story about what is truly important in life.

Explorations	Areas of Emphasis
Half of Everything	Number Patterns Problem Solving
Jars of This and Jars of That	Measurement Number Estimation Problem Solving Mathematical Language
Penny Savers	Measurement: money Number Statistics Estimation

Half of Everything

Areas of Emphasis

- Number
- Patterns
- Problem Solving

Group Size

- Pairs of students

Teacher Materials

- jar picture master (page 61)

Student Materials

For each pair

- tub of beans
- jar picture sheet

Introduction

Say: "The little girl helped her mother at the Blue Tile Diner. Do you remember what she did with the money Josephine gave her?" (She put half of it in the jar.)

Procedure

Initiate a class discussion of what half means. Then divide the class into pairs. Give each pair a tub of beans and a copy of the jar picture. Say: "We will pretend the beans are pennies for today's exploration. Let's say you get paid 12 cents for working at the Blue Tile Diner. You save half of everything you earn. How much would you save today?" Let each pair decide on a strategy to solve the problem. Ask the groups to share their answers and strategies. Show students how to record the amount in the jar picture. First have them explore, placing half of the beans in the jar. Then have them record the amount in the jar.

Continue with another amount: "The next evening Josephine gave the little girl 18 cents for helping at the diner. How much did she put in the jar?" Again let the pairs choose a strategy and share the results with the class. This time ask them if they chose the same strategy as the last time. Which strategy worked best? Direct the discussion to a comparison of various strategies. Tell students to record the amount saved in the jar. Continue until the students have five amounts recorded or until their interest diminishes.

Extension

"How much money is in your jar?" Pairs may use calculators but must check their answers using another tool. They may use the beans, an equation, and so on.

7¢ + 9¢ + 5¢ + 6¢ + 11¢ = 38¢

We used tiles to check our work.

Jar

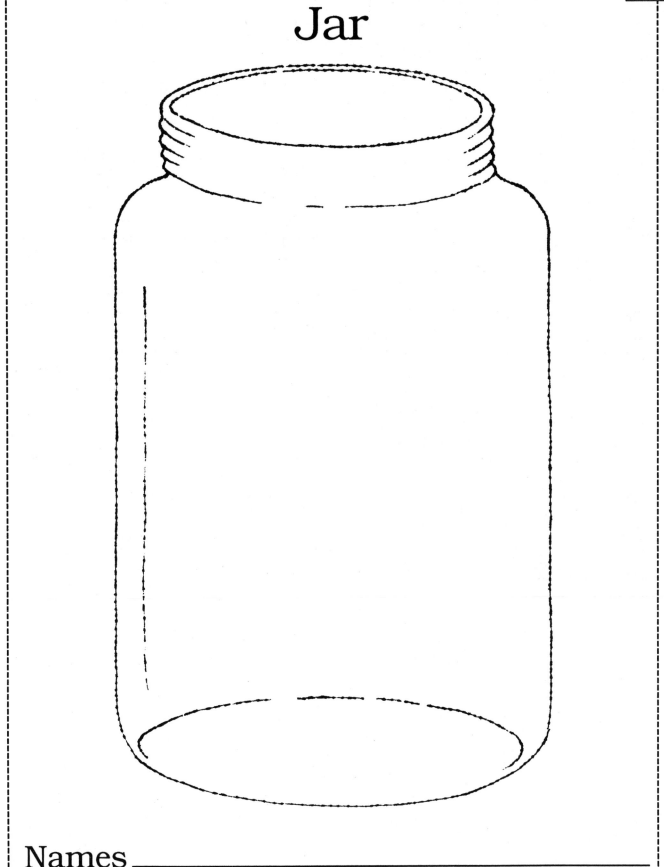

Names _____

Jars of This and Jars of That

Areas of Emphasis

- Measurement
- Number
- Estimation
- Problem Solving
- Mathematical Language

Group Size

- Whole class

Teacher Materials

- 1-gallon glass jar
- unicubes

Student Materials

For each group
- 1-gallon glass jar (optional)
- objects such as pasta shells, clothespins, and tiles (optional)

Introduction

Ask: "When will the family know it is time to go out and buy a chair?" (When they can't get another single coin into the jar, they are going to take out all the money and buy a chair.) Show the class a 1-gallon glass jar and say: "It would take a lot of anything to fill a jar as big as this one." Ask: "How many unicubes do you think it will take to fill this jar?"

Procedure

You can either record the estimates on the chalkboard or have students write them in their math journals. Tell them everyone will partici-pate in filling the jar, and it will be important to keep track of the number of cubes in the jar. Ask for suggestions on how to stay organized. If you do not get any suggestions, your class will benefit from seeing an organizational strategy modeled. Instruct everyone to get five unicubes. They should not snap them together. Students should call out the count as each student places his or her five unicubes in the jar: 5, 10, 15, 20.... When everyone has put five unicubes in the jar, record the total on a chart.

Cubes in Jar

Round	Cubes Each	Total
1	5	75

"How many unicubes should we each put in this next round?" Ask for reasons to support their decisions: "I think we should only get two because we almost filled the jar, and if we each get five, all of us won't be able to put unicubes in." Repeat the procedure.

To summarize, have students write a short description of the process and results of the exploration in their math journals. They should include the chart in the write-up.

Extension

Divide the class into small groups of 3–5 stu-dents. Give each group a gallon jar, paper, and a pencil. Assign each group a specific item such as pasta shells, clothespins, or tiles. Tell stu-dents they must first make a group estimate on the number of items needed to fill the jar. They must have a reason for their final choice: "We decided that since clothespins are bigger than unicubes the number would be smaller and 79 is smaller than 126." Allow time for each group to share this first group decision. This is an opportune time to learn mathematical strategy and language from one's peers.

After students have shared their group esti-mates, let them fill the jars. Use this time to watch, listen, take notes, and assess. Which groups are discussing, keeping track of the count, making decisions? Guide those in trouble with suggestions rather than directives.

Let each group present its jar. Students may want to ask the class for estimates before they present their findings. Encourage students to ask questions and make comments. Keep the jars and results of the explorations on display for a while to encourage further discussion.

Penny Savers

Areas of Emphasis

- Measurement: money
- Number
- Statistics
- Estimation

Group Size

- Whole class

Teacher Materials

- 1-gallon glass jar

Introduction

Say: "The family in *A Chair for My Mother* decided that when the jar was filled they would go and buy a comfortable chair. They had a family goal. Let's start our own savings jar. Let's start saving pennies. We will have a lot of time to decide on how we will spend the money."

This is an exploration that will extend over a long period of time and can be managed many different ways. There will be opportunities to include estimation, number, graphing, regrouping, recording, and problem solving in this open-ended situation. The depth will be your decision.

Procedure

Begin with a discussion of a "legal" or acceptable penny for the jar. Pennies that students are given, earn, or find are legal. Keep a record of the total in the jar. Calculate the new amount each time students contribute. You could also build a graph based on every time you have enough for a dime, a quarter, or a dollar.

As the jar fills up, the class will be able to make more accurate estimations of the final amount. This will make for more realistic decisions about how to spend the money. You may want to encourage students to integrate this project with a social science unit. Connecting mathematics instruction to other curriculum areas is the goal of an integrated program.

During a long-term project like this, students will gain a new perspective on their own learning. Skills that were at first difficult will become easy. They will gain a greater depth of competence in all the mathematical areas presented.

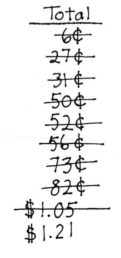

Total
6¢
27¢
31¢
50¢
52¢
56¢
73¢
82¢
$1.05
$1.21

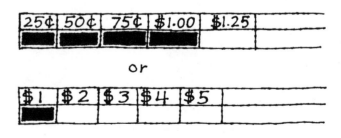

25¢	50¢	75¢	$1.00	$1.25		
■	■	■	■			

or

$1	$2	$3	$4	$5		
■						

"A Lost Button" and "Spring" from Frog and Toad Are Friends

by Arnold Lobel

• •

Frog and Toad are friends. They are kind, humorous, and capable of incredible acts of valor, foolishness, and, best of all, friendship. In "A Lost Button," Toad loses one of his jacket buttons during a walk with Frog. The two retrace the entire trip in hopes of finding the lost button. Many hours later, the only thing they have to show for their efforts is very sore feet. In the story "Spring," Frog tries to coax Toad to leave his winter bed and enjoy the wonders of spring.

Explorations	Areas of Emphasis
Is This Your Button, Toad?	Logic: attributes Mathematical Language
A Smile a Day	Patterns Mathematical Language Organization Skills Number
The Bullfrog Jump	Measurement Problem Solving Mathematical Language Number Estimation

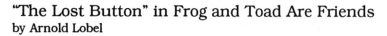

Is This Your Button, Toad?

Areas of Emphasis

- Logic: attributes
- Mathematical Language

Group Size

- 3–5 students

Teacher Materials

- selection of buttons

Student Materials

For each group
- small tub of buttons

Introduction

Tell students that you have many buttons that may be identical to Toad's lost button, which was white, had four holes, and was big, round, and thick. They will have to decide whether each button really is identical to Toad's button.

Before starting the activity, prepare tubs of buttons for the groups. Most of the buttons should be white and have some of the attributes of Toad's buttons (that is, four holes, big, round, thick). Include in each tub two or three buttons that fit all five attributes of Toad's button.

Procedure

Select some buttons that do not follow any of the rules of Toad's missing button. Show students one of the buttons and ask: "Could this be Toad's button?" Require that they give you a reason why it cannot be Toad's button. Make a list on the chalkboard or a large piece of butcher paper as they tell you why the various buttons can not be Toad's button. "That can't be Toad's button because it isn't white." "That can't be Toad's button because it's small, and Toad's button has to be big." "Toad's button was thick and that button is thin, so it can't be his button." As soon as you have all five attributes listed and the class has read them, you are ready for the second part of this exploration.

Toad's Button

White
4 holes
Big
Round
Thick

Divide the class into groups of 3–5 students. Give each group a tub of buttons. Tell students that each tub includes at least two buttons that fit all five rules for Toad's button. They must find those buttons. Remind them to make sure everyone in their group participates and that they listen to the ideas, opinions, and suggestions of all the members of their group.

Let students direct their own exploration. Use this time to assess the members of each group. If a group has lost direction, guide them with careful questions rather than with directives.

The final step of this exploration involves each group sharing its findings with the class. At this point, you and the rest of the class can ask students to explain why they chose particular buttons and why they didn't choose some of the others in their tub. Try to involve all members of each group in this final presentation.

Extension

Let the groups sort buttons according to any attributes that they select. I have done this many times and am always amazed at how inventive and enthusiastic students are.

Another variation is to let group members take turns selecting one attribute and having the rest of the group try to guess what it is by selecting buttons and asking "Does this button follow your rule?" If the button does follow the rule, it stays in the IN pile, if it does not follow the rule it goes in the OUT pile. I would advise that the student who is selecting the rule must write down the attribute on a piece of paper to avoid any last-minute changes.

A Smile a Day

Areas of Emphasis

- Pattern
- Mathematical Language
- Organization Skills
- Number

Group Size

- Pairs of students

Teacher Materials

- 8 ½" x 11" paper
- scissors

Student Materials

For each pair
- 8 ½" x 11" paper
- scissors
- calculator

Introduction

Say: "Toad never wants to get in such a blue mood again. He realizes that it is very important to keep a positive attitude. He decides to start every day with a smile. He announces to Frog, 'I've made a decision! I will draw and paste a smiling sun on my calendar every morning. I have a lot of work to do. I will have enough pieces for the entire year if I fold and cut this paper six times.'"

Procedure

Divide the class into pairs. Fold an 8 ½" x 11" sheet of paper in half and then cut it on the fold line. Ask: "Will Toad have enough pieces of paper for an entire year after six folds? How many folds and cuts do you think he needs to make?" Never skip this part of the lesson. As students discuss this situation, record their responses and predictions. Ask them how they decided on their predictions. Some students will be able to articulate their rationale; others will not. The student who answers with "I don't know" or "I can't explain why" will learn from the student who can express a reason. Don't judge. The class discussion must be viewed as a safe time to express ideas. Interacting with each other helps each student to clarify his or her ideas, view another perspective, and "talk mathematics." Your role is to make sure that the class has a clear understanding of the problem and the information that is pertinent. Direct the discussion to the fact that a year has 365 days. "When will Toad know that he has enough pieces of paper?" "Tell me everything you know about a year." "Toad needs a piece of paper for every day in a year. How many days is that?"

Say: " I am going to show you a mathematical strategy called a T-Table. It will keep you organized and make it easier to see patterns as you work on this problem." Students should discuss how they will share the folding, cutting, counting, and recording. Give each pair of students a piece of 8 ½" x 11" paper and scissors.

As you make the first entry on the T-Table, use precise language: "After the first fold and cut, I have 2 pieces of paper." Ask the class what headings would be appropriate for the columns. We decided on Fold and Pieces when I did this lesson. After you and the class make the second fold and cut and record the results, instruct the pairs to continue with the activity until they find the results for six folds and cuts.

FOLD	PIECES
1	2
2	4
3	8
4	16
5	32
6	64

● ●

As the pairs continue independently, monitor their progress. When a problem arises, ask careful questions rather than giving direct instructions. If you see a pair with only one student working, you might ask how they are sharing the responsibilities of the exploration. Remind students to check each other's work. When all the pairs have made the six folds and cuts, bring the class back together. Now ask them: "Was Toad correct in his estimation? Do you have enough pieces of paper to make suns for an entire year?" At this point they may change their original estimates. They now have enough information to make better estimates. Direct the discussion to what changed as each successive fold and cut was made. It will get more difficult to cut the stacks and count and recount the pieces of paper.

Now is the time to bring students' attention to the patterns in the left and right columns of the T-Table. After they have discovered and discussed the "counting-by-ones pattern" in the left column and the "double-the-previous-number pattern" in the right column, tell them they may use a calculator to find out how many folds and cuts Toad will have to get to make suns for the whole year. (9 folds and cuts; 512 pieces of paper) Ask them why they think it might be better to use a calculator to continue this investigation. Ask pairs that finish early to figure out how many extra pieces of paper Toad will have after he draws enough suns for a year. (512 − 365 = 147 leftover pieces of paper) They can solve this any way they choose.

Extensions

- Ask: "How many tires are on seven bikes?" Have pairs use a T-Table to organize the information and see if there are any patterns. "The column on the left will be Bikes; the column on the right will be Tires."

- Ask: "How many tires are on seven tricycles?" Again tell pairs to organize the problem using a T-Table. Then have them write about the patterns they found.

The Bullfrog Jump

Areas of Emphasis

- Measurement
- Problem Solving
- Mathematical Language
- Number
- Estimation

Group Size

- 3–4 students

Teacher Materials

- bullfrog master (page 71)
- masking tape
- lily pad master (page 72)

Student Materials

For each group
- lily pad sheet
- unicubes
- string
- scissors
- one-inch tiles (optional)

Introduction

Say: "There are many kinds of frogs, and one of the biggest and most powerful is the bullfrog. A bullfrog is an incredible jumper. An adult bullfrog can jump twenty times its length." Be sure students understand the concept of *length*. Duplicate and cut out the model of the adult bullfrog (page 71) and show it to students. Place a strip of masking tape on the floor. Tell students that their goal for today's lesson is to make a prediction. Ask: "If an adult bullfrog jumps from this line, where will it land?"

Procedure

Divide the class into small groups. Give each group a lily pad, and have each group member write his or her name on the lily pad and then cut it out. Make the bullfrog available for students to measure. Each group must estimate where the bullfrog will land, and place its lily pad there. Tell students they may use any of the mathematical tools you have provided—unicubes, string, paper, scissors—to assist them in this problem. The most important part of this lesson is the strategy planning and discussion

in which the groups must participate. Working as part of a team, students will realize that everyone's contribution is essential to the success of the project. The small-group approach changes the role of the teacher to a facilitator. Encourage group discussion and help students identify the important aspects of the problem.

When all the groups have come up with an estimate and put their lily pads in place, bring the class together. Each group should now share how it came up with its estimate. What facts did students use; what tool helped them solve the problem? "We measured the bullfrog with the unicubes and made a tower of the cubes. Then we flip-flopped the tower 20 times. We put our lily pad on the last flip." "Candi, Ben, and I measured the bullfrog with the string. We cut the string and used that to find out where the frog would stop. We are sure that we are very close."

Say: "I will now place the bullfrog on the starting line and have it jump twenty times its length." Remind students that the most important part of the exploration wasn't how close they came, but how they planned their strategy.

Extension

Ask: "How many inches do you think the bull-frog jumped?" Show students a one-inch tile. Ask: "How many one-inch tiles do you think it would take to cover the distance?" Let everyone write an estimate in a Guess Box. (A Guess Box is a square that is divided into two triangles. The top triangle is used to record an estimate; the bottom triangle is used to record the actual count.) Now give everyone a one-inch tile. Tell students they will place one-inch tiles from the starting line to where the frog landed after jumping twenty times its length. As they take turns placing the tiles, they should keep track of the number. When everyone has placed one tile, give students an opportunity to change their estimates. Give everyone another tile and proceed until the tile line reaches the bullfrog.

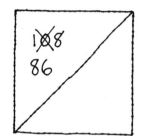

Guess Box

Top △ : estimates
Bottom △ : count

Bullfrog

Lily Pad

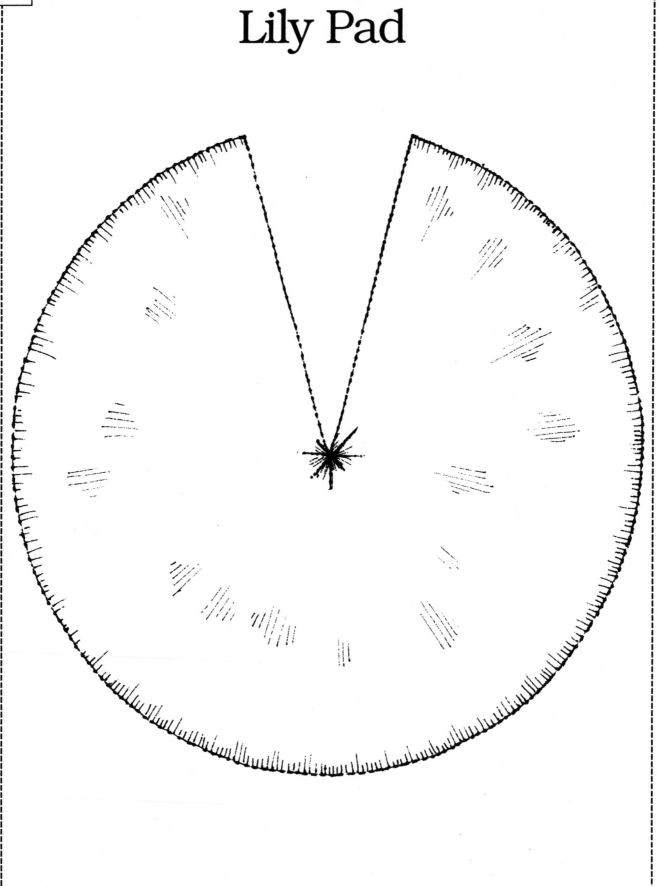

MATH EXPLORATIONS BASED ON

Who Sank the Boat?

by Pamela Allen

• •

A cow, a donkey, a sheep, a pig, and a mouse decide to go out in Mr. Peffer's boat. As each animal gets in the boat, the reader is asked, "Who sank the boat?" This is a delightful story that teaches the principles of balance.

Explorations	Areas of Emphasis
Mystery Numbers	Measurement Number
Cooperative Measurement	Estimation Measurement Number Group Strategy Mathematical Language
Spin and Tally	Probability Number: fractions Recording Skills Mathematical Language

Mystery Numbers

Areas of Emphasis

- Measurement
- Number

Group Size

- Pairs of students

Teacher Materials

- balance scale
- tiles or cubes
- tissue

Student Materials

For each pair
- balance scale
- tiles or cubes

Introduction

Say: "The animals in the boat were fine as long as they were balanced. Does anyone know what *balance* means?" If you have a see-saw in your playground, use it to explain balance. Let students find partners who will balance the see-saw with them. Ask them why certain people will balance the see-saw. Another activity is trying to balance a ruler over the edge of a desk. Have students turn the ruler over so that they can't see the numbers.

Procedure

Divide the class into pairs of students, and give each pair a balance scale. If you have only a few balance scales, then model the exploration for the whole class and set up centers for follow-up by student pairs.

Place between 5 and 10 tiles in one of the buckets on the scale. Do not let the class see how many you put in, and quickly place a tissue over the top of the bucket. Tell the class: "When you balance the scale, you will know my mystery number." Let students place one tile at a time in the empty bucket. Always let them put in at least one too many so that they can see how the scale becomes unbalanced again. Model this procedure at least four times. Let students take turns choosing a "mystery number" and directing the exploration. Limit them to 25 tiles.

Extensions

- Organize centers so students can experience using the balance scales in small groups. Challenge them to find objects in the room that weigh 5 tiles, 10 tiles, and 20 tiles. Tell them to record their findings with small pictures of the objects. Then have them start a graph. If some students have made the transition from nonstandard to standard units of measurement, provide them with metric or U.S. customary weights for this activity.

- Have students choose any object in the room, estimate its weight, and then weigh it. Have students record the weights on a chart.

		guess	weigh
Paper cup		50	10 grams
Jelly beans		Timmy 100	100
Eraser		50	39
Sticker book		Martha 100	3
bag of dice		100	Jennifer 46
SHOE		Kristen & Jennifer ?	158

Cooperative Measurement

Areas of Emphasis

- Estimation
- Measurement
- Number
- Group Strategy
- Mathematical Language

Group Size

- 4–6 students

Student Materials

For each group

- miscellaneous objects
- paper strip
- balance scale

Introduction

This exploration must be preceded by "Mystery Numbers" (page 74). Divide the class into small groups of 4–6 students. Tell the groups to choose something in the room that can fit into a balance scale bucket and draw a picture of it. Have each group choose a total of five objects.

Procedure

Have each group place its objects in a sequence according to estimated weight, from lightest to heaviest. Groups may use any strategy to estimate weight except the balance scales. Encourage students to work together closely. After they have placed the objects in sequence, have them record their estimates by placing the pictures in the same order on a strip of paper. They should not glue them down at this point.

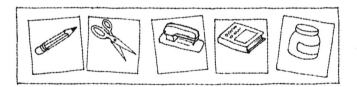

When the groups have finished, bring the class together and have students share how they made their decisions. Make a record of the different strategies they used. Then tell them to go back to their groups and weigh each object with the balance scale and tiles. Tell them to record the weight on each picture and adjust the position of the pictures on the strip of paper if necessary. At this point they may glue the pictures onto the paper. Again bring the class together to discuss the discrepancies between their estimates and the actual weights.

| 7 Tiles | 12 Tiles | 24 Tiles | 26 Tiles | 41 Tiles |

Spin and Tally

Areas of Emphasis

- Probability
- Number: fractions
- Recording Skills
- Mathematical Language

Group Size

- Whole class
- Pairs of students

Teacher Materials

- animal spinners (pages 78–80)

Student Materials

Per pair
- 1 red circle
- 1 black circle

Introduction

Say: "I have some spinners that show the animals from *Who Sank the Boat?* We are going to make some predictions based on these spinners."

Procedure

Arrange the class in a circle on the floor. Place the Mouse and Sheep Spinner (page 78), which is divided into ¼ and ¾, in the middle of the circle. Tell the class: "Everyone is going to spin an animal. The animal that the spinner lands on the most will sink the boat. Who do you think will sink the boat?" Record their predictions on a tally sheet. This is also a good time to introduce recording with a fraction. You must use good mathematical language for this introduction; for example: "Of the 26 students, 11 predict that the mouse will sink the boat. Of the 26 students, 15 predict that the sheep will sink the boat."

As each student spins, record the outcome on another tally sheet. After this first round, tell the class that they may change their predictions before you all spin again. This time, ask them why they are either changing or staying with their original prediction. I recommend spinning more than once because the more you spin the more pronounced the outcome will be. This is called the *Law of Large Numbers.*

After the second round of spins, ask: "How many times have we spun?" (52 times) How many times did we land on the mouse? (17 times) How many times did we land on the sheep? (35 times) How could we record this information mathematically? (mouse $^{17}/_{52}$, sheep $^{35}/_{52}$) Why do you think we landed on the sheep more often? What part of the circle belongs to the sheep? What part of the circle belongs to the mouse?"

```
PREDICTIONS FOR MOUSE/SHEEP

MOUSE    ||||| |||||        11
             |              ——
                            26

SHEEP    ||||| |||||        15
         |||||              ——
                            26
```

Divide the class into pairs of students, partner A and partner B. Give A a red circle and B a black circle. Have students fold and cut the circles in half and then into fourths. They will need to trade pieces so that they can make the Mouse and Sheep Spinner. Direct the discussion to how many pieces the sheep and mouse cover. "The sheep has 3 of the 4 pieces. Mathematicians write that as ¾. The mouse has only 1 of the 4 pieces, or ¼."

Extensions

■ Show students the Sheep and Cow Spinner (page 79). Say: "Trade pieces with your partner to make this spinner. Write the fraction." Continue with the same format as in the Mouse and Sheep Spinner: predict, spin, tally, and discuss results.

■ For the Pig, Cow, and Sheep Spinner (page 80), have students work in groups of three students to make the circles in three colors. Ask: "How would you write the parts of this spinner like a mathematician?" (½, ¼, ¼) They should be much more sophisticated by now. Require that they give reasons for their predictions. If your class is ready, have them express the prediction as a fraction: $^{13}/_{26}$ will be the pig, $^6/_{26}$ will be the cow, and $^7/_{26}$ will be the sheep.

Mouse and Sheep Spinner

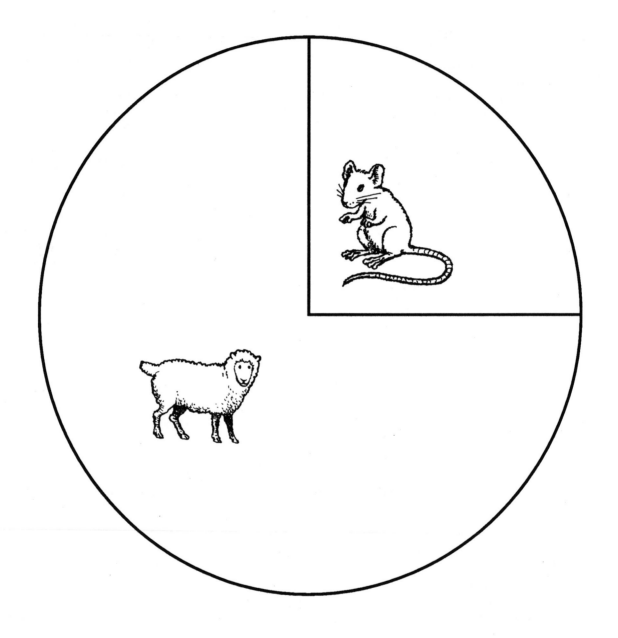

Sheep and Cow Spinner

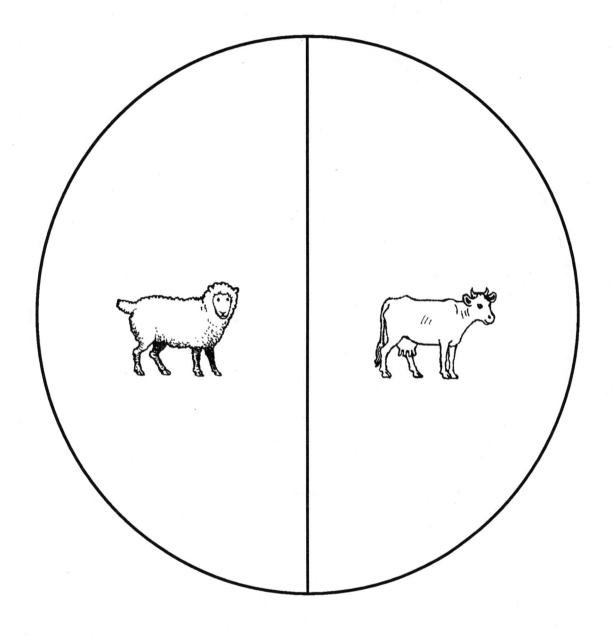

Pig, Cow, and Sheep Spinner

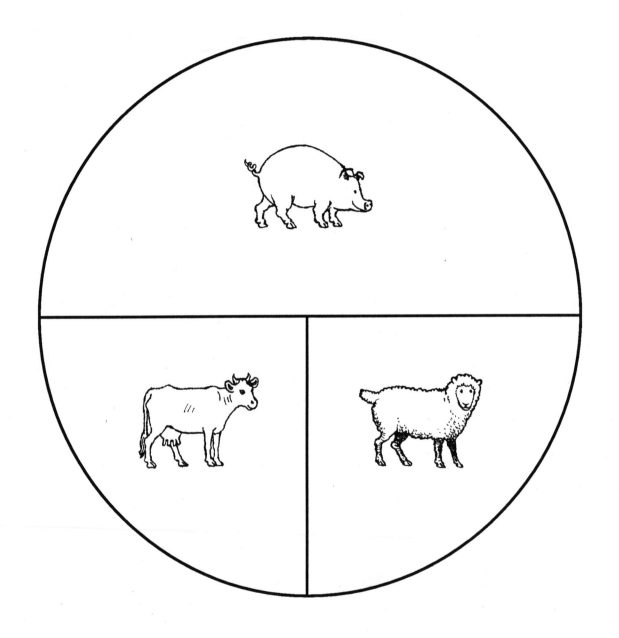

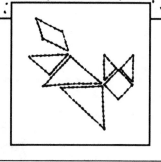

MATH EXPLORATIONS BASED ON

Grandfather Tang's Story

by Ann Tompert

· ·

Grandfather Tang and Little Soo like to make shapes with their tangram puzzles. Grandfather Tang makes two foxes out of the pieces and tells a story of two fox friends, Chou and Wu Ling, who can change into other animals. As he tells the story, Grandfather Tang makes the animal shapes with the tangram pieces.

Explorations	Areas of Emphasis
Free Explorations	Geometry
Metamorphosis	Geometry Mathematical Language
Tangram Challenge	Geometry

Free Explorations

Area of Emphasis

- Geometry

Group Size

- Individuals

Teacher Materials

- tangram pattern master (page 83)
- the book *Grandfather Tang's Story*

Student Materials

For each student

- tangram puzzle
- oak tag
- scissors
- self-lock bag

Introduction

If you do not have enough tangrams for the entire class, have students use the tangram pattern on page 83 to trace and cut tangram pieces out of heavy stock oak tag. Laminating the pieces increases their life. Give each student a self-lock bag in which to store his or her tangram pieces.

Say: "Later this week, I am going to read you a Chinese story about fox fairies. According to Chinese folklore, fox fairies live for eight hundred to a thousand years and can change themselves into any animal. In the story, the storyteller uses tangrams to show the animals that the fox fairies change into."

Procedure

Bring the class together in a circle on the floor. Show the class the seven pieces of the tangram puzzle. Explain: "A tangram begins with a square. It is divided into seven standard pieces. You can arrange the seven pieces to create a picture of anything you want." Place the tangram pieces on the floor, and model how to make a fox. "I am going to use all seven pieces to make one of the fox fairies from the story." Make a fox using the diagrams in the book as a reference. Say: "Now *you* make a fox." Let the children explore with this first animal. Let them share their efforts with their classmates.

After students have shared, say: "There is also a dog, hawk, crocodile, goose, rabbit, squirrel, turtle, goldfish, and lion in this story." List the animals on a chart or the chalkboard so that students can refer back to the list. "See how many of the animals you can make with your tangrams. Maybe you'll be able to make something that isn't on the list. Draw a picture of everything you build in your math journal."

Bring the class together in a circle on the floor. Let each student make his or her favorite tangram picture to share with the class. Let students trace their pictures on paper, label them, and display them on a bulletin board.

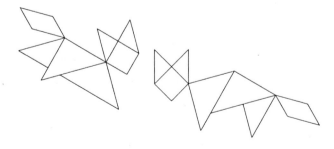

Tangram Pattern

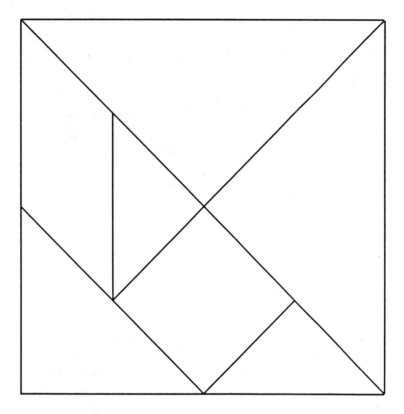

Metamorphosis

Areas of Emphasis

- Geometry
- Mathematical Language

Group Size

- Pairs of students

Teacher Materials

- the book *Grandfather Tang's Story*

Student Materials

For each student

- tangram puzzle

Introduction

Divide the class into pairs. Say: "I am going to read *Grandfather Tang's Story*. There are two fox fairies in this story. One is named Chou, and the other is Wu Ling. I will stop each time either Chou or Wu Ling uses its power to change into another animal. One of you will be Chou and your partner will be Wu Ling. You will change your tangram pieces into the new animal. You will be helping me to tell the story."

Procedure

Give each student a tangram puzzle (see template on page 83). Let students decide who will be Chou and who will be Wu Ling. Start by having each student place his or her pieces into the form of a fox.

Then begin reading the story. The first page has Wu Ling changing into a rabbit.

"'I can change myself into a rabbit as quick as a wink,' boasted Wu Ling." Make sure that students realize that only the student who is Wu Ling makes a rabbit. Give students ample time to make a rabbit. Partners may help each other if asked.

"'Not bad,' said Chou. 'But watch me do better than that.' And before Wu Ling could blink, Chou changed from a fox into a dog!" Remind the class that only the students who are Chou make a dog.

Continue with this format. Do not rush to finish the book in one sitting. Give students ample time to make each animal. Encourage teamwork and verbal sharing. I recommend that you read the story many more times. Varying the partner groups encourages more sharing of knowledge, language, and technique.

When you have finished reading the book, review the sequence of the story with the entire class. Generate a list of the transformations of Wu Ling and Chou. Have students record this information in their math journals. Have pairs practice telling the story with their tangrams. When they are ready, schedule times for them to tell Grandfather Tang's story in other classes.

Extension

Encourage student pairs to create new adventures for Chou and Wu Ling and present their stories to the class.

Tangram Challenge

Area of Emphasis

- Geometry

Group Size

- Individuals in groups of 3–4

Teacher Materials

- animal outline masters (pages 86–96)
- the book *Grandfather Tang's Story*

Student Materials

For each student
- tangram puzzle
- animal outlines

Introduction

Say: "You have had some experience in making animals using tangram pieces. I'm going to give you outlines of the animals in *Grandfather Tang's Story*—your challenge is to fit all seven tangram pieces correctly into each animal outline."

Procedure

Divide the class into groups of 3–4 students. Give each student a tangram puzzle (see pattern on page 83) and a set of animal outlines (pages 86–96). Each member of the group must complete an animal before another one is chosen. Encourage students to share how they solved each picture. After you have checked a solution, have the student sign his or her name on the back of the picture. (The solutions can be found on the pages in *Grandfather Tang's Story*.)

Extension

Have groups choose a storybook that could be told using tangram pictures. The group members must first find an appropriate book and then work together to translate it into a tangram story. Some suggestions include *The Grouchy Ladybug* by Eric Carle, *Who Sank the Boat?* by Pamela Allen, and *Mr. Gumpy's Outing* by John Burningham.

Fox

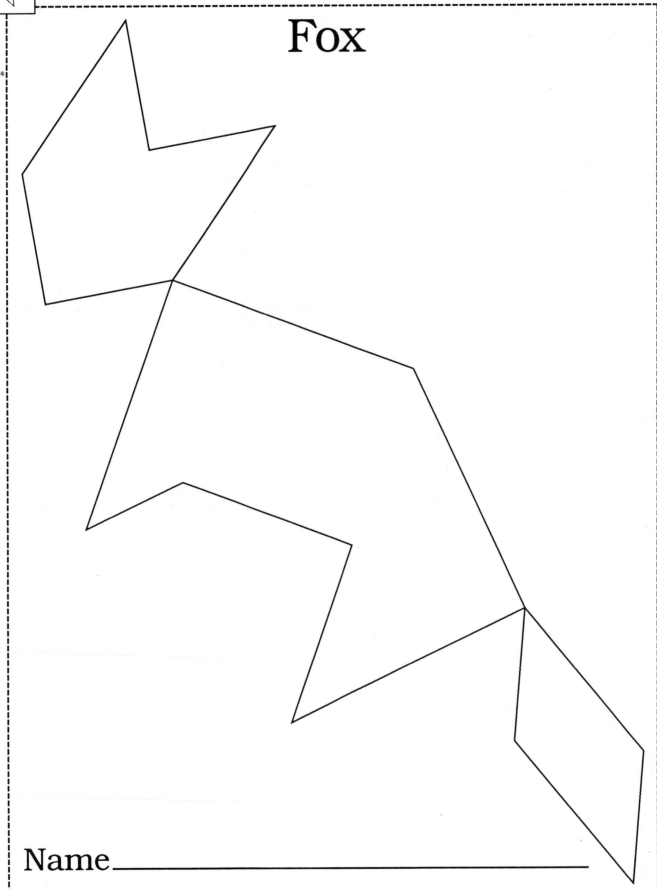

Name_____

Fox

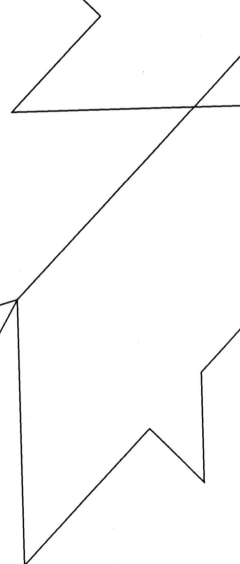

Name _____

Rabbit

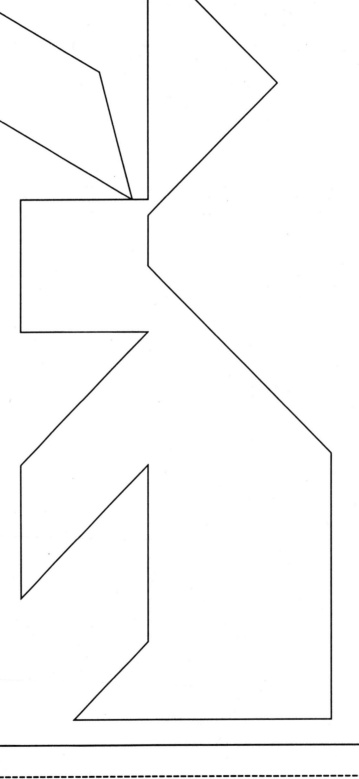

Name _____

Dog

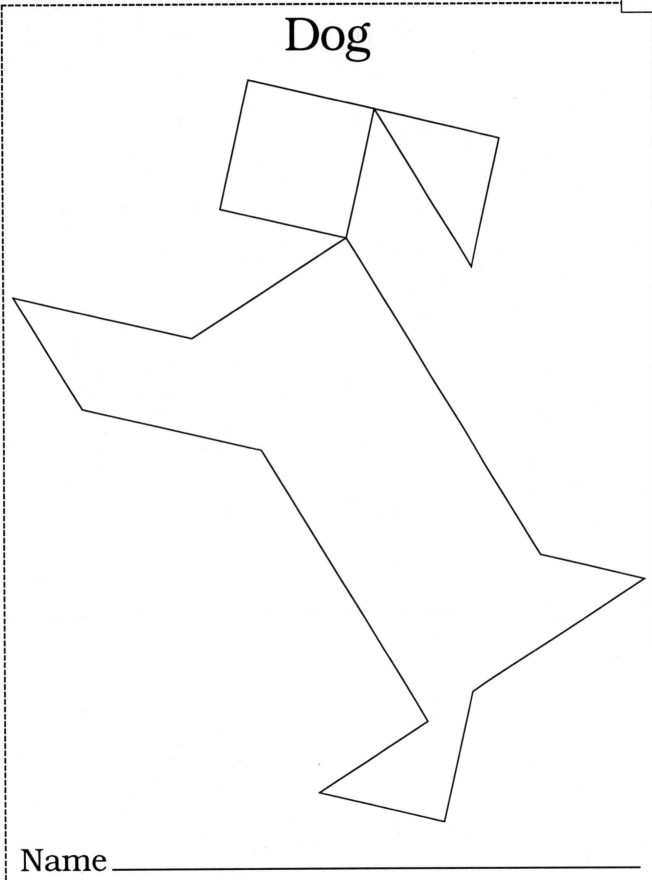

Name _____

Squirrel

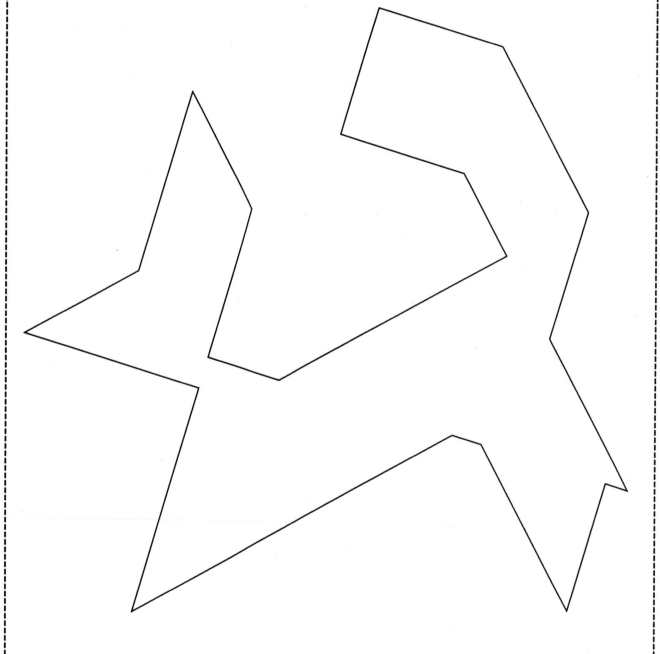

Name _____

Hawk

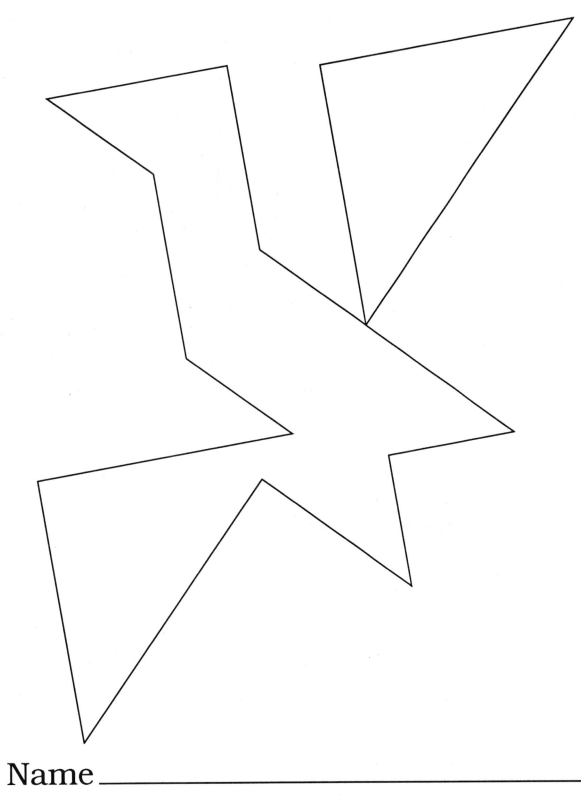

Name _____

Turtle

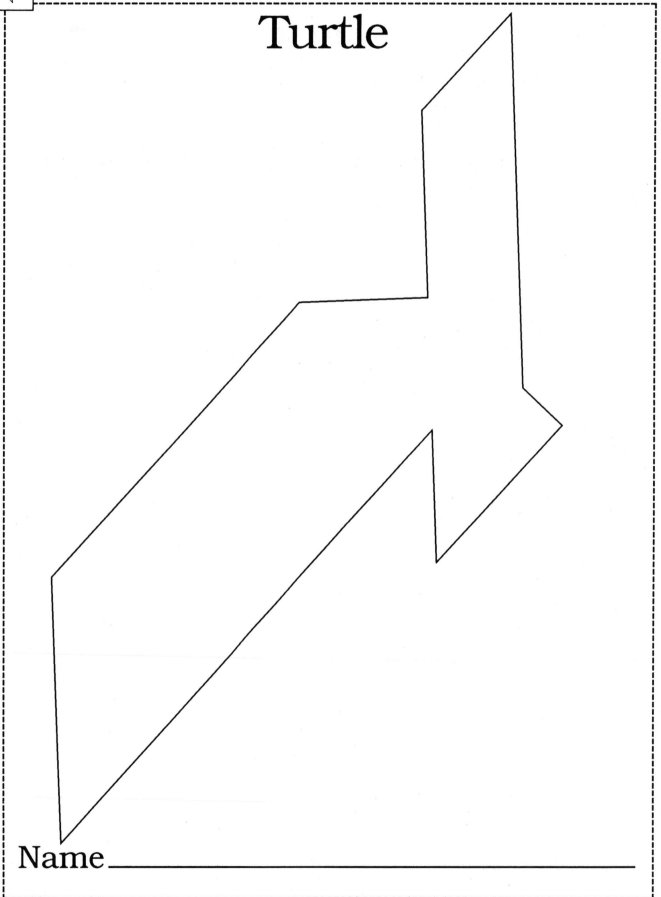

Name _____

Crocodile

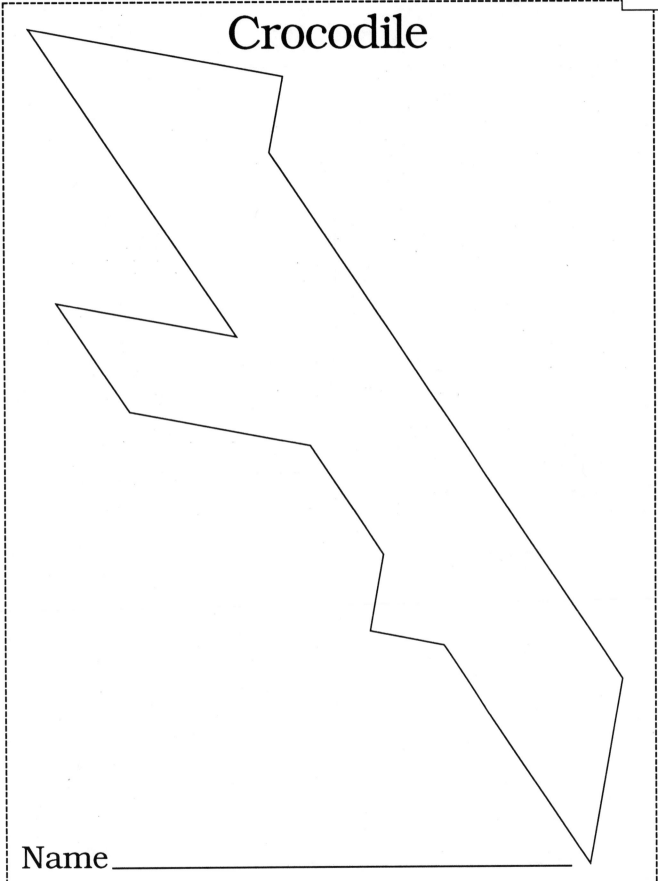

Name _____

Goose

Name _____

© Dale Seymour Publications

Goldfish

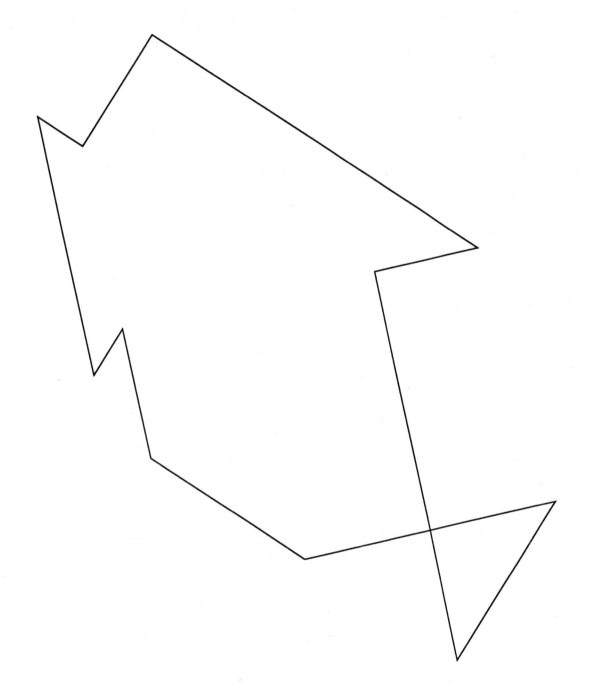

Name _____

Lion

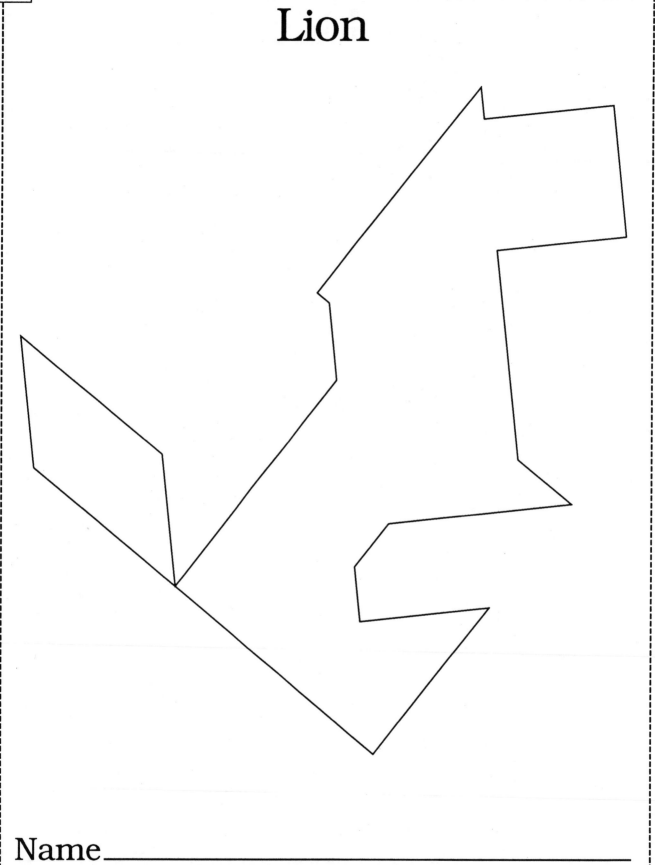

Name_____

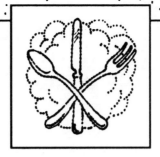

Cloudy with a Chance of Meatballs

by Judi Barrett

The tiny town of Chewandswallow was like many other towns except for the weather. Three times a day, it rained things like soup, juice, mashed potatoes, and hamburgers. Life was very easy for the people of Chewandswallow, since everything they ate came from the sky. But one day the weather took a turn for the worse, and awful things began to happen. The town began to fear for its life. Something had to be done, and fast.

Explorations	Areas of Emphasis
Ham, Spam, and Radishes	Logic: attributes Mathematical Language
The Weather Report	Measurement: calendar Patterns Mathematical Language
Temperature Log	Measurement: temperature Statistics: graphing Mathematical Language

Ham, Spam, and Radishes

Areas of Emphasis

- Logic: attributes
- Mathematical Language

Group Size

- Pairs, or groups of 3 students

Introduction

Tell students you are going to play a game inspired by *Cloudy with a Chance of Meatballs.* "Every month, only foods that followed a specific rule fell from the sky. I will tell you some of the foods that fell during a month, and you have to figure out the rule for that month."

Procedure

Divide the class into pairs or groups of three students. They may discuss the problem only with the others in their group. Say: "Last January in Chewandswallow, hamburgers and hot dogs fell from the sky but *not* scrambled eggs." Begin a YES and NO chart on the chalkboard. Put hamburgers and hot dogs under the YES column and scrambled eggs under the NO column. (Do not tell students at this point that the rule for January is "foods that have meat in them.") Ask if anyone would like to guess what other foods may have fallen from the sky in January. If the food follows the rule, say: "Yes, that food follows the rule for January." List it

under the YES column. If it does not follow the rule, say: "No, that food doesn't follow the rule for January." List it under the NO column. Do not allow students to tell you what they think the rule is; they can only show you that they know what the rule is by naming foods that follow the rule. If someone gives the rule, the game is over!

If students have trouble naming correct foods, you may give them a few more foods that do and do not follow the rule. After you give an example, allow sufficient time for students to discuss in their groups the new food and what the rule might be.

Repeat the format for other months of the year. Do at least three months together. When the students become comfortable with the format, let the groups make up a rule for a month. Have them write their rule and list 12 foods that do and do not follow the rule. Let them try their rule with other groups. Display the rules for each month with students' art of the foods that do and do not follow the rules.

The Weather Report

Areas of Emphasis

- Measurement: calendar
- Patterns
- Mathematical Language

Group Size

- Individuals

Student Materials

For each student

- calendar page
- crayons

Introduction

Remind students: "The people of Chewand-swallow listened to the weather report every morning and night just like some of us do. There were predictions about what the weather would bring in the following days. We are going to become weather reporters and forecasters by watching for weather patterns!"

Patterns are everywhere. Children who are encouraged to look for patterns...begin to understand how mathematics applies to the world in which they live. Such connections...foster the kind of mathematical thinking that serves as a foundation for the more abstract ideas studied in later grades. (NCTM *Standards*, page 60)

Procedure

In this exploration, students sit together and share information but work independently to create their own record of the lesson. Give everyone a calendar page of the previous month. Say: "On the first day of last month in Chewand-swallow, it rained cinnamon toast." Show them the box on the calendar that refers to the first day of the month. Begin a discussion such as: "It was the first Tuesday. It's in the third column." Tell students to draw a picture of the weather (cinnamon toast) in the appropriate box on the calendar. Ask: "What was the weather on the second day of the month?" Ask students to give reasons for their predictions. Do they really have enough information to make a sound prediction?

If it is appropriate for your class to do an AB

pattern, tell them the following day it poured strawberry yogurt. Again find the corresponding square on the calendar, prompt a discussion of that date, and have everyone draw a picture of the weather—strawberry yogurt.

Continue the lesson with whatever pattern you think is appropriate for your class. A simple AB pattern (cinnamon toast, strawberry yogurt, cinnamon toast, strawberry yogurt, etc.) is appropriate for students who are in the initial stages of recognizing and extending patterns. This is a good place to begin assessing your class. Always promote discussion of the calendar in terms of how to describe a particular date, along with how to extend the pattern.

As students begin to recognize the pattern, let them continue it on their own. You can assess their progress by asking what the weather will be on a particular date. "What kind of weather do you forecast for October 24?" "Do you see any patterns within your pattern?" Some patterns will produce interesting diagonals.

October

Sun	Mon.	Tues.	Wed.	Thurs.	Fri.	Sat.
		1	2	3	4	5
6	7	8	9	10	11	12
13	14	15	16	17	18	19
20	21	22	23	24	25	26
27	28	29	30	31		

Extensions

■ Have students draw a month's weather by listening to your calendar clues: "On the first Monday of October, it snowed fruit salad"; "On the third Thursday, it drizzled baked beans all day"; "On the last day of October, there were huge clouds of waffles."

■ Let students create their own weather patterns. They will enjoy sharing their patterns with others. In the student art opposite, Michelle realized she made a mistake in her ABB pattern when she noticed the diagonal lines. Wednesday, March 4, should have been part of the diagonal line. She said, "I'm supposed to have a pattern within a pattern!"

Michelle	**March**					
Sun.	Mon.	Tues.	Wed.	Thurs.	Fri.	Sat.
1 ☁	2	3	4	5	6	7 ☁
8	9	10 ☁	11	12	13 ☁	14
15	16 ☁	17	18	19 ☁	20	21
22 ☁	23	24	25 ☁	26	27	28 ☁
29	30	31 ☁				

Temperature Log

Areas of Emphasis

- Measurement: temperature
- Statistics: graphing
- Mathematical Language

Group Size

- Individuals

Teacher Materials

- large temperature log master (page 102)
- small temperature log master (page 103)
- outdoor thermometer

Student Materials

For each student

- 15 copies of small temperature log sheet

Introduction

Say: "A meteorologist studies weather patterns in order to predict future weather. We are going to start a weather log."

Procedure

This is best as an individual project. Students will each have a permanent record of the exploration. Before beginning the lesson, make a copy of the large and small temperature log masters (pages 102 and 103) and fill in this month's dates. Then make 15 copies of the small log sheet for each student.

Show students the large drawing of the thermometer. Explain why the mercury rises with the temperature. Discuss how to read the number scale. (This would be a good time to use an overhead projector.)

The first morning, let students look at a thermometer outside the room. Record the outdoor temperature on the large thermometer picture. Circle today's date on the calendar, and record

the temperature in the temperature box. Then have students do this on their log sheets. Use descriptive language for the date: "Today is the first Monday. What column is today in? How many Mondays are in this month?"

Continue this routine daily for the entire month. Ask for predictions about the next day's weather. Make a class line graph of the temperature information you compile. Have students participate in recording the daily temperatures. Say: "Who can tell us what the temperature was on April 13? What day of the week did it fall on? Can you show us where that temperature would be on this graph?"

Extensions

- Start a display of weather graphs that the students find in various newspapers. Have them sort them into graph types: circle, line, bar, and so on.
- Schedule a trip to a weather station, or have a guest speaker.

Temperature Log

Today is _____

Sunday	Monday	Tuesday	Wednesday	Thursday	Friday	Saturday

Temperature:

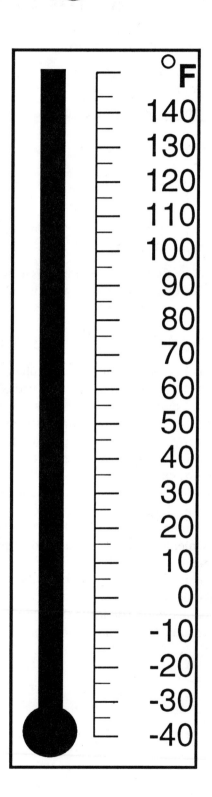

Today is _____

Sunday	Monday	Tuesday	Wednesday	Thursday	Friday	Saturday

Temperature:

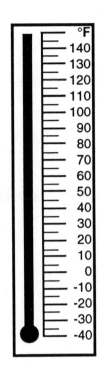

Today is _____

Sunday	Monday	Tuesday	Wednesday	Thursday	Friday	Saturday

Temperature:

Knots on a Counting Rope

by Bill Martin Jr. and John Archambault

· ·

A blind Native American boy learns from his grandfather how to live successfully in his sightless world. Each time the grandfather tells the story of the boy's birth, he ties another knot on a counting rope. As the knots increase, so does the boy's confidence and ability.

Exploration	Areas of Emphasis
A Necklace of Value	Number
	Problem Solving
	Mathematical Language

A Necklace of Value

Areas of Emphasis

■ Number
■ Problem Solving
■ Mathematical Language

Group Size

■ 3–4 students

Teacher Materials

■ red and blue beads
■ string

Student Materials

For each group
■ 10 red and 10 blue beads
■ string
■ crayons

Introduction

Say: "What would the grandfather do each time he told the boy the story of his birth? Yes, he would put another knot on the counting rope. I am going to start a counting rope. Red beads will have a value of two storytellings. Blue beads will have a value of only one storytelling." Note: Any color beads can be used, but limit this first exploration to two colors.

Make a necklace of red and blue beads. Limit the necklace to five or fewer beads. Ask the class if they know how many storytellings the necklace is worth. Record the values for the beads on a chart that everyone can see.

Value Chart

Red = 2   Blue = 1

As you string the beads, ask questions: "What is the value of this bead? How many story tellings is my necklace worth so far?" Summarize this introduction by asking the class if they know how many storytellings the completed necklace is worth. Show the class how to record the final necklace and its value.

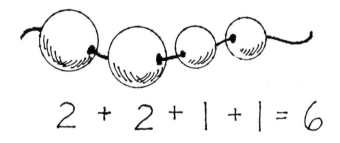

$$2 + 2 + 1 + 1 = 6$$

Procedure

Divide the class into small groups of 3–4 students, and supply each group with red and blue beads and string. Tell the groups to make a necklace with five beads. When they are finished, ask them the value of their necklace. Provide enough time for students to share their strategies for addition. Have them record this first necklace by drawing the necklace and writing its corresponding number sentence.

Let students make a few more necklaces of specific lengths. Each time, ask them to tell the value of their necklace and to record the results.

●●●

Extension

Students should now be comfortable with the materials and the format of this exploration. Give them a problem to solve: "I made a necklace that has 6 beads and has a value of 11. Make my necklace." Encourage students to discuss the problem first with the rest of their group. Review the results in a whole-class discussion. Continue with variations of this format—7 beads with a value of 9; 7 beads with a value of 11; 8 beads with a value of 14; and so on. Each time, review the strategies with the class and have groups make a record of the necklace.

The value chart for the beads can be based on color, shape, or type of bead and can be adjusted for any level. I have used this type of format for first through fourth grades. It is a wonderful assessment activity and also fosters persistence.

MATH EXPLORATIONS BASED ON

Curious George Rides a Bike

by H. A. Rey

Curious George is a good but curious monkey. He lives with the man with the yellow hat. To celebrate their third year together, Curious George gets a new bicycle. His adventures on his new bike range from delivering newspapers to working in a circus.

Explorations	Areas of Emphasis
An Odd Job for George	Patterns Number Mathematical Language
Anniversary Adventures	Patterns Problem Solving
Build a Better Boat	Geometry Number Measurement
A Boat a Page	Number Patterns Problem Solving

An Odd Job for George

Areas of Emphasis

- Patterns
- Number
- Mathematical Language

Group Size

- Pairs, or groups of 3 students

Student Materials

For each pair or group

- counters
- 100 chart
- crayons

Introduction

Say: "Curious George and the newsboy eventually become friends. George is a good assistant. One morning, the newsboy asks George to deliver papers to the odd-numbered houses on the street. George needs our help."

Procedure

Divide the class into pairs or groups of three students. Supply each group with counters, a 100 chart, and crayons. Tell students that the houses on Brattle Street are numbered from 1 to 51. Remind them that George is to deliver papers only to the odd-numbered houses. Say: "One way to see if a number is odd or even is to divide that number of counters into 'partners.' If there are no counters left over, the number is even; if there is a counter left over, the number is odd." Point out that 1 counter cannot be divided into "partners." It is odd.

Record 1 as odd by coloring the number 1 yellow on the 100 chart. Say: "Color the odd numbers on the 100 chart yellow when you find them. Color the even numbers that you find orange." Continue testing the numbers with the class until students feel confident.

Bring the class together for a discussion when they are finished. Did students see any patterns? Do they know which numbers are even? Could they predict whether a number is odd or even without testing it? Say: "Tell me something about all the odd numbers. Tell me something about all the even numbers." Responses may include: "I found that all the even numbers have 0, 2, 4, 6, or 8 in the singles place." "The odd numbers all have 1, 3, 5, 7, or 9 in the singles place." "There was an AB pattern on the 100 chart when I tested the numbers."

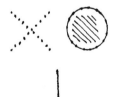

1

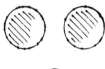

2

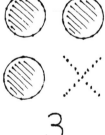

3

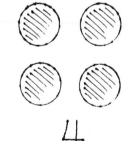

4

Extension

Have students write letters to George, telling him how to find out whether a number is odd or even.

Dear George,
the way to tell if a number is odd take some Beans or tiles and look at the number and get out that many Beans or tiles and pair them up if theres a Bean or tile left than that means its odd george your a curies monkey and funny monkey.

Dear George,
The way you could learn how to tell a odd number from a even is to put numbers In pairs. Lets take the number 5 divide it buy 2 and if there's one lef its odd if there isen't it's even. Now George you should try one for your self.

Dear George,
I heard you are having trobble figern out the differnts betwin odd and even! Maby I can help you, lissen. the numer one is odd because it has no parmter but the number two is even because it has a panter and so on now do you get it? I hope so!

Anniversary Adventures

Areas of Emphasis

- Patterns
- Problem Solving

Group Size

- 3–4 students

Student Materials

For each group

- counters
- paper

Introduction

Ask: "When do you usually give people presents?" Discuss the various occasions: birthdays, holidays, anniversaries. Continue: "Curious George has lived with the man with the yellow hat for three years. That is a lot of time. If George got a dollar for every month he has lived with the man, would he have enough money to buy a bicycle?"

Procedure

Divide the class into small groups of 3–4 students, and distribute the counters. Before allowing students to use the counters, tell them to discuss the information that is important to solve the problem. They should record the information. Let the groups share their important information. Review the number of months in a year. You will be surprised how many students will not remember this information even though they learned it in kindergarten! Information is remembered when it is needed to solve problems. Suggest that students name each month.

Once they know that there are 12 months in one year, they are prepared to solve the problem. Let them choose any mathematical tool except a calculator, although they can check their work with a calculator. Use this time to observe the various approaches. I saw students recite the months of the year as they used the counters. The use of tally marks was another strategy, as well as addition (12 + 12 + 12). Remind students to be prepared to share their strategies by writing an account or explaining them to the class.

Extension

Ask: "Does Curious George have enough money ($36.00) to buy a bicycle?" Provide catalogs, bicycle brochures, and quotes from local stores. Let each student or group decide on a bicycle. "How much more money, if any, would he need? How many years would that be for George?"

Build a Better Boat

Areas of Emphasis

- Geometry
- Number
- Measurement

Group Size

- Individuals

Teacher Materials

- the book *Curious George Rides a Bike*
- newspaper
- tub of water (optional)

Student Materials

For each individual

- sheet of newspaper
- gram cubes, tiles, or unicubes (optional)
- balance scale (per group or class) (optional)

Introduction

Say: "Curious George actually made a boat out of a newspaper! He is a very talented monkey. If George can make a boat out of a newspaper, so can we!"

Procedure

Follow the instructions on pages 17 and 18 of *Curious George Rides a Bike* to make a boat. Make several practice boats before trying it with the class.

Give each student a sheet of newspaper and explain how to make the boat. As they fold the newspaper, call attention to the changing shapes of the emerging boat. Ask: "How many triangles do you see? How many rectangles?" Make diagrams on the chalkboard for those who need more than verbal instruction. (Studies show that, on the average, only 40 percent of students are auditory learners.) You might want to tell them that making your first boat was difficult, but with practice, making a boat got easier and easier.

A third-grade class that participated in this exploration started making boats at home. The students used various kinds of paper. They came to school with a flotilla of boats! Their teacher was excited to see her students so engaged. Experiences like this validate the importance of exploration math lessons.

Extensions

- Ask: "How many cubes can our boats hold?" Record students' predictions on a chart. I used gram cubes for this part of the exploration, but tiles or unicubes will also do. Fill a tub with enough water to float a paper boat. Have the class count off as each student puts a cube into the boat. Stop when the boat appears ready to sink. Have students compare their estimates with the actual number of cubes the boat held. Older students can work in small groups. Instruct students to record the procedure and results in their math journals.

- Provide students with a balance scale and have them weigh the number of cubes that the boat held in the Extension above. Then tell them to find objects in the classroom that the boat might hold without sinking. Make a chart with the headings "Boat Can Hold," "Will Sink the Boat." Tell students to draw a picture of their object, weigh it, write the weight on the picture, and then paste the picture in the appropriate column on the chart.

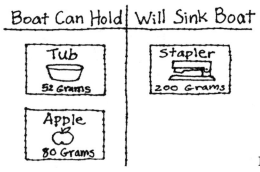

A Boat a Page

Areas of Emphasis

- Number
- Patterns
- Problem Solving

Group Size

- 3 students

Teacher Materials

- 100 chart
- crayon

Student Materials

For each group

- counters
- portion cups
- 100 chart
- crayon

Introduction

Say: "Curious George made boats, and more boats, and even more boats. He didn't stop making boats until he used up all the newspapers. He made so many boats that he couldn't count them. It looked like an entire paper boat fleet." Ask: "How many boats did Curious George make that day? I have information that you can use to answer this question."

Procedure

Divide the class into groups of three students. Supply each group with counters and portion cups. Say: "Each newspaper had nine pages. George made a boat with each page. Use counters to show how many boats George made with the first newspaper." Instruct the groups to discuss this information before doing anything. Tell them to put the counters for that number of boats in a portion cup.

Model recording the information on a T-Table. Use simple mathematical language as you build and use the table: "The left column will tell us how many newspapers George has used, and the right column will tell us how many boats he has made." Have students show with their portion cups how many boats George made with the second newspaper. The groups should start their own tables to record this exploration. Encourage them to comment on the emerging pattern: "The numbers in the left column are increasing by 1. The numbers in the right column are increasing by 9."

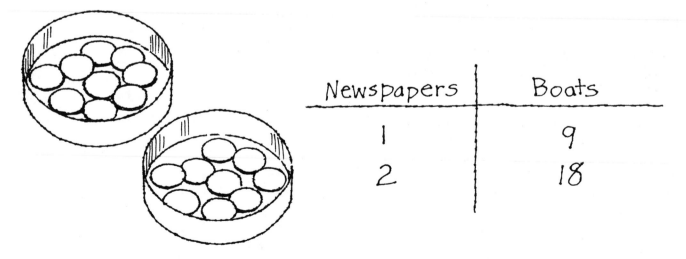

Newspapers	Boats
1	9
2	18

Give each group a 100 chart. Say: "Now I will show you another way to record this information. Because George made nine boats from the first newspaper we will color in the number 9 on the 100 chart. What number should we color in next?" Direct the students in a discussion on the next number. The emerging pattern will be another way for the students to make predictions.

Share the last bit of information students need: "George used eight newspapers that day." Direct the groups to use their counters to show how many boats George made out of eight newspapers. Remind them to use the portion cups so that the beans won't get mixed up. Encourage the groups to share what they did with the beans. Ask: "How many boats did George make with three newspapers? How do we record this new information on the table? How do we record this on the 100 chart?" Require that students to use good mathematical language.

Record the results on the table and 100 chart with the class. Direct their attention to the emerging pattern on the 100 chart. This is the same pattern that is on the right side of the T-Table.

1	2	3	4	5	6	7	8	9	10
11	12	13	14	15	16	17	18	19	20
21	22	23	24	25	26	27	28	29	30
31	32	33	34	35	36	37	38	39	40
41	42	43	44	45	46	47	48	49	50
51	52	53	54	55	56	57	58	59	60
61	62	63	64	65	66	67	68	69	70
71	72	73	74	75	76	77	78	79	80
81	82	83	84	85	86	87	88	89	90
91	92	93	94	95	96	97	98	99	100

Ask the class: "Which mathematical tool did you like working with the most (counters and T-Table, or the 100 chart)? Why?" Keep students in their groups for a prewriting discussion of five to ten minutes. Then have them write in their math journals.

Extension

This activity is appropriate for a center. Have students use counters and portion cups to find out how many boats George could make with 20 newspapers and record the results in a T-Table or 100 chart.

MATH EXPLORATIONS BASED ON

The Grouchy Ladybug

by Eric Carle

• •

The grouchy ladybug is looking for someone to fight, no matter how big. From sunrise to sunset, the ladybug has nothing but hostile encounters. Then the ladybug meets its match and learns the value of friendship.

Explorations	Areas of Emphasis
Share and Share Alike	Number: division and fractional parts Mathematical Language
Lunch	Number: subtraction Mathematical Language
Comparative Language	Mathematical Language: comparative language for measurement Logic: attributes
Geometric Animals	Geometry Mathematical Language
Bigger Than a Ladybug	Measurement: scale, proportion, and area Mathematical Language

Share and Share Alike

Areas of Emphasis

- Number: division and fractional parts
- Mathematical Language

Group Size

- Pairs of students

Teacher Materials

- leaf master (page 116)

Student Materials

For each pair
- 4" x 5" sheet of paper
- green crayon
- leaf sheet

Introduction

The concept of division should be introduced with concrete materials in real-world situations before it is introduced symbolically. This is the beginning of an operational sense of numbers. Recognizing when it is appropriate to use a specific operation must begin with concrete explorations.

Ask: "Do you know how the grouchy ladybug greets its neighbors? 'Do you want to fight?' That's how the grouchy ladybug greets its neighbors. The ladybug spends a long day arguing with neighbors and ends up a very hungry and tired ladybug. If the grouchy ladybug had known about sharing, its day would have been a lot more successful and enjoyable."

Procedure

Divide the class into pairs. Give each pair a 4" x 5" piece of paper and a green crayon. Have pairs make aphids by coloring both sides of the paper green and tearing it into bits that will represent aphids. Then give each pair a leaf sheet. Say: "This leaf is divided into two parts that are the same size. You and your partner are ladybugs. You are both very hungry but very polite. You agree to share all the aphids you find." Use the term *divide* as well as *share*. Students will soon realize that the terms mean the same thing.

Each pair will have a different number of aphids. Tell the pairs to count the aphids and record the number. Ask: "Why does each pair of students have a different number of aphids?"

Say: "Now it's time to share the aphids. Write your name on one side of the leaf. With your partner, divide the aphids and put one half on each side of the leaf." (Some pairs of students will have an odd number of aphids. Let each pair decide how to handle this by either dividing the aphid in half or setting it aside and calling it "one extra.") Let each pair share the results of its investigation. Discuss the term *one half*. If it is appropriate for the age and skill level of your students, introduce the symbol ½.

Continue: "You are all such friendly ladybugs! You may give some of your aphids to the pair on your left." Students shouldn't tell how many they are giving or ask how many they are receiving. Have pairs count the aphids, record the number, divide the aphids, record the results, and share the findings.

> We got 32 aphids. We shared them. I got 16. Beth got 16.
> by Beth and Paulo

Extension

Ask students to discuss how they would share 24 marbles equally with a friend. They may use any mathematical tool to solve the problem. They should record the process and results of their investigation in writing or with a picture.

Leaf

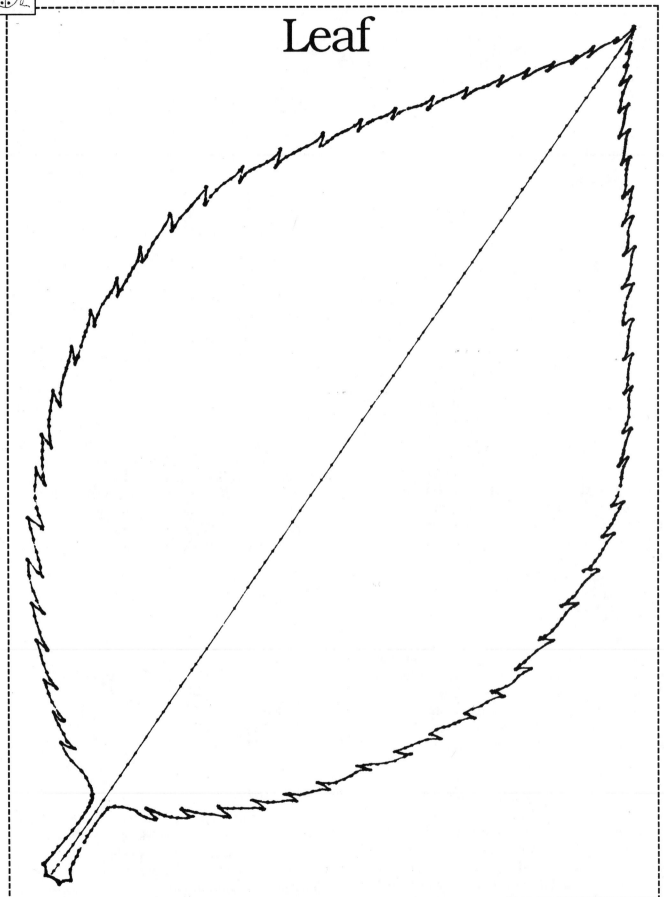

Lunch

Areas of Emphasis

- Number: subtraction
- Mathematical Language

Group Size

- Whole class

Teacher Materials

- leaf master (page 116)
- stapler

Student Materials

For each student

- five 3" x 6" paper strips
- leaf sheet
- 5 beans, unicubes, or paper bits
- construction paper

Introduction

Students come to school knowing many words that are associated with numbers. You want to build on this language and connect it to mathematical symbols. Language is the basis for learning. Because mathematical language involves the use of symbols, students must be given many opportunities to build a concrete understanding. Many activities must be provided to ensure this transition to symbolic language.

Say: "You are ladybugs—very polite ladybugs! You are just about ready for lunch. You land on a rosebush leaf and see five luscious aphids."

Procedure

Give each student a leaf sheet and five beans, unicubes, or bits of paper to use as aphids. Tell them to place five aphids on their leaves.

Say: "You really aren't very hungry since you had a hearty breakfast. You eat only one aphid." Tell students to remove one aphid from their leaves. Ask someone to explain what has happened in the story so far.

Say: "Now it's time to record what has just happened." Have the students write the number sentence on a paper strip as you tell the story: "There were 5 aphids on the leaf. I ate 1 of

them. Now there are only 4 aphids on the leaf $(5 - 1 = 4)$. Ask for volunteers to tell the whole story again as they point to the numbers and symbols. Get as much language participation as you can before going on.

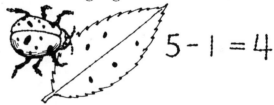

Say: "Time for another juicy aphid!" Repeat the procedure, having students record the number sentence on a paper strip $(4 - 1 = 3)$. Continue until all the aphids are gone. To assess students, say: "Hold up the number sentence you wrote that tells this part of the story: 'There were 3 aphids and I ate 1 of them. Now there are only 2 aphids on the leaf.'" Continue with each story part and number sentence at random. Have students come up and tell a story using one of the number sentences they wrote. Let them make covers for the storybooks and staple the pages together.

The Grouchy Ladybug
by Eric Carle

Extension

On another day, present the same investigation with a new twist. Say: "Today you are a very hungry ladybug. You spent the entire morning looking for aphids and were unsuccessful. You just spotted a lilac bush with a lot of aphids. You land on a leaf that has 12 fat aphids." Have the students place 12 aphids on their leaves. Continue: "You are so hungry that you forget your manners and pop 2 aphids in your mouth." Continue with this pattern (–2). As before, stress the language and symbol connection with each number sentence. Ask students for predictions about how many aphids will be left to eat. Then test the predictions with the concrete activity. It is better to keep this type of activity short and repeat it many times. The next time you direct the activity, mix up the number of aphids that are eaten each time. You don't want students to think the number subtracted always has to be the same. Most of all, keep it fun. The most learning occurs when students are stress-free and happy.

Comparative Language

Areas of Emphasis

- Mathematical Language: comparative language for measurement
- Logic: attributes

Group Size

- 4–6 students

Student Materials

For each group

- twelve 4" x 4" pieces of paper
- crayons
- glue
- paper strip

Introduction

Prepare for this lesson a day ahead. Divide your class into groups of 4–6 students. Give each group twelve 4" x 4" pieces of paper. Have them draw each creature the grouchy ladybug met on a piece of paper. Remind students to share the responsibility and label the drawings. Then have students glue the animals on a paper strip in the sequence in which they met the ladybug. This sequence strip will be the mathematical tool for the comparative explorations.

Procedure

Assemble the class into their groups with their sequence strips. Tell students there are some important rules for this exploration:

- Listen carefully to the clues.
- Answer in complete sentences.

Give students the first clue: "I am bigger than a praying mantis and smaller than a lobster. Who am I?" Repeat the clue. Circulate around the room. There will always be a group that needs some direction or a few provoking questions to get them on the right track. Tell the groups to record the question and their answer to it. Let each group share its response to the clue. Praise good comparative language.

Give students another clue: "I am bigger than a lobster and smaller than a hyena. Who am I?"

This time there are two possibilities. Again stress teamwork and good language. Ask students to record the question and their answers and then share their findings with the class.

Continue: "I am bigger than a stag beetle and smaller than a boa constrictor. Who am I?" Continue: "I am bigger than a hyena and smaller than whale. Who am I?"

Extensions

- Let the groups make up a clue for a creature. They should write the clue and the possible answers and share the clue with the class.

- Let the groups choose six items in the room, line them up according to size, and make as many comparisons as possible: "The stapler is bigger than the pencil and smaller than the book." This provides an assessment opportunity.

- Introduce the class to Venn diagrams and tell them to use their sequence strips to illustrate some of the comparisons.

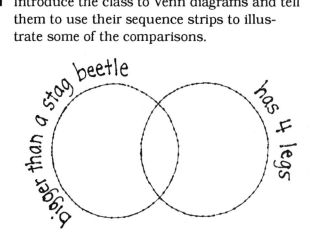

Geometric Animals

Areas of Emphasis

- Geometry
- Mathematical Language

Group Size

- Individuals

Teacher Materials

- geometric shape patterns master (page 121)

Student Materials

For each student
- geometric shape patterns
- scissors
- glue
- paper

Introduction

Say: "Eric Carle is the writer and illustrator of *The Grouchy Ladybug.* Every illustrator chooses a specific style for his or her book. But you don't have to be an artist to make the animals in this book. Today we're going to make the animals from different geometric shapes.

Procedure

This is an individual exploration. Supply your students with the geometric shape patterns. Instruct them to cut out the shapes and use them in any combination to construct the various animals in *The Grouchy Ladybug.*

Extension

Have students choose one of the animals they made and write directions on how to make it. Encourage them to share their animals and directions with the class.

I made a ladybug.
I cut a circle in 2 for the body.
A small circle for the head.
Skinne rectangles for the legs.
Long rectangles for anntenas.

Geometric Shape Patterns

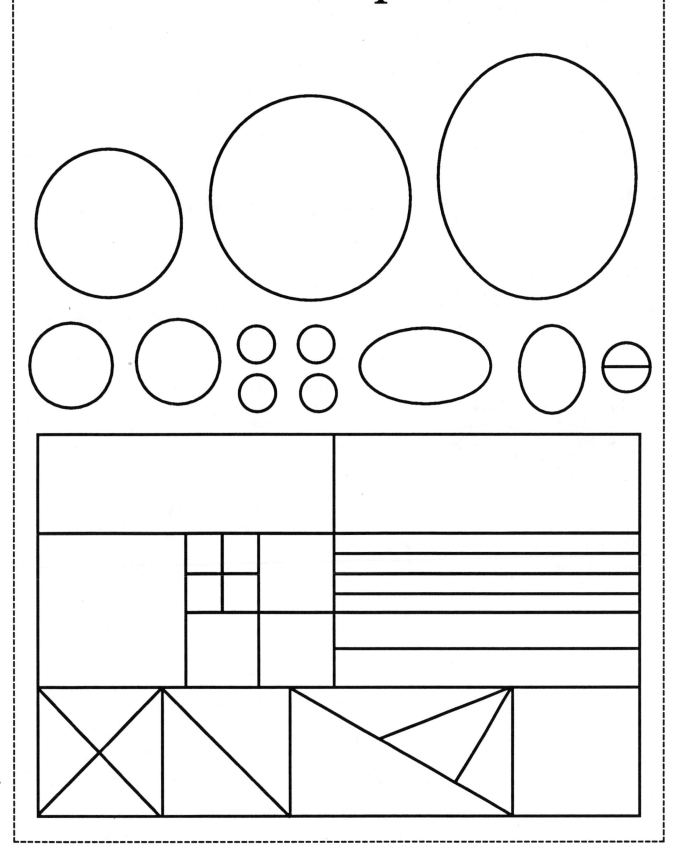

•••

Bigger Than a Ladybug

Areas of Emphasis

■ Measurement: scale, proportion, and area
■ Mathematical Language

Group Size

■ Individuals in groups

Student Materials

For each student

■ 1-cm graph paper
■ crayons
■ scissors
■ tape
■ string
■ coat hanger
■ ruler (optional)

Introduction

Tell the class: "The ladybug met a new animal each hour. There was a pattern. Did you notice what was happening?" (The animals got bigger and bigger and bigger.)

Procedure

Have students sit together in groups so that they can share information. Supply each student with sheets of 1-cm graph paper and crayons. Say: "The ladybug fits inside one of the squares on your graph paper." Write the information on the chalkboard. Continue: "The ladybug meets a yellow jacket first. How many squares do you think the yellow jacket needs?" Record the information students give. Elicit the possible height and width of the yellow jacket. Read all the information back to the class. Have each student draw the ladybug and the yellow jacket on the graph paper. Students should record the number of squares they used to draw the insects. You may want to give them recording sheets.

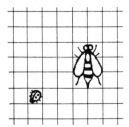

ladybug – 1 square
yellow jacket
        – 6 squares
stag beetle –

Say: "The ladybug met a stag beetle next and then a praying mantis." Discuss the size differences between these insects and the ladybug and yellow jacket. Repeat the procedure: discuss the information, record it, read it back, and have students draw it on the graph paper and record the area. This is a good point to end this part of the exploration. Instruct the students to cut out the insects, tape string to the back of each one, and tie them onto a coat hanger. This is the beginning of a "Grouchy Ladybug mobile."

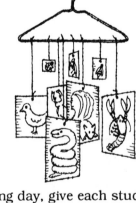

The following day, give each student another piece of graph paper and begin a discussion of the next two animals, the sparrow and the lobster. Ask: "How many squares do you think the sparrow needs on your graph paper? The lobster?" Record students' comments and read them back to the class. Ask: "How much bigger is the sparrow than the praying mantis? Will the sparrow cover twice as many squares? How big an area will you need to draw the lobster?"

After the animals are drawn, students can add the pictures to their mobiles.

Repeat the procedure until the class has drawn the ladybug, yellow jacket, stag beetle, praying mantis, sparrow, lobster, skunk, and boa constrictor.

Extensions

■ Direct a class discussion with questions and comments: "If we want to draw the rest of the animals the ladybug met, we must make some changes. How many squares would we need to draw a whale? I have a solution. We will start a new mobile. The hyena will fit in one square of the graph paper, and we will compare the rest of the animals to the hyena." Repeat the procedure using the new scale.

■ Supply each student with a ruler, paper, and a pencil. Ask: "Did anyone notice what happened to the print in the storybook *The Grouchy Ladybug*?" (It increased in size as the animals got bigger and bigger.) Say: "We are going to do something similar today." Model measuring and drawing the first set of lines. Say: "Draw a straight line with your ruler. Now measure ½ inch above the line. Do this above the beginning and the end of your line, and mark each measurement with a dot. Draw a line to connect the two dots. You now have *parallel* lines—they are exactly ½ inch apart and will never meet. Print your name in the space between the two parallel lines—use the entire space." Circulate and provide assistance as needed.

Continue: "We are now going to draw two more parallel lines, but this time we will increase the space between the lines by ½ inch. How big will the space between the lines be? Yes, it will be 1 inch. After you draw your parallel lines, print your name in the space. Be sure to fill the entire space." Have students continue to draw parallel lines that increase by ½ inch each time. Their names will get bigger and bigger.

MATH EXPLORATIONS BASED ON

Millions of Cats

by Wanda Gág

• •

This is the story of a very old man and a very old woman who long for an addition to their family. The very old woman tells the very old man that she wants a cat to keep them company. He goes out to find the most beautiful cat in the world and returns with "hundreds of cats, thousands of cats, millions and billions and trillions of cats."

Explorations	Areas of Emphasis
Picture This	Number Mathematical Language Mathematical Symbols
Half for You, Half for Me	Number Mathematical Language
Graph That Cat!	Statistics: graphing Number Mathematical Language
Secret Ballot	Statistics: sampling, data collection, analysis, and graphing Number Mathematical Language
Fraction Mats	Number: fractions Problem Solving Mathematical Language

Picture This

Areas of Emphasis

- Number
- Mathematical Language
- Mathematical Symbols

Group Size

- Pairs of students

Teacher Materials

- story pictures master (page 127)
- cats master (page 128)

Student Materials

For each student
- story pictures
- cat pictures
- scissors
- paste

Introduction

This story can be used to create many beginning number situations. Students have enough language to describe mathematical situations. This type of exploration gives students an opportunity to add mathematical language and symbols to their vocabulary. As they develop mathematical understandings, they will begin to understand the symbols and language of mathematics.

Tell the class: "Today we are going to have some cat adventures, and record them as a mathematician would."

Procedure

Divide the class into pairs. Students in each pair are to help each other. Give each student a sheet of story pictures and a set of cats. Tell students to cut out the individual cats. Direct their attention to the first story picture. Say: "There are two cats on the hill. There is one cat under the tree." Tell the students to show this on their pictures by pasting the cats in place. Then have them tell you as much as they can about the picture.

Say: "I am going to show you how a mathematician would record this story: There are two cats on the hill: 2. There is one cat under the tree: +1. There are three cats in the picture: = 3."

Have each student write the number sentence on his or her picture. Allow the students to come up and tell the whole story about this picture and its number sentence.

Have students look at the second story picture. Say: "There are four cats hiding in the tree." Have students place their cats in the tree. "One of the cats gets very thirsty and jumps out of the tree." Have students place one cat on the ground. "How many cats are in the tree now?" Have students explain what happened and tell how they know that there are only three cats in the tree now. Then have them paste down the cats. Again show them how to write the story as a mathematician would, and let them share.

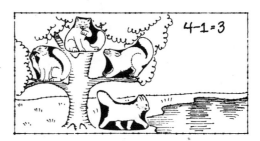

Have students look at the third story picture. Say: "There are five cats resting under the tree. Four cats run away. How many cats are still under the tree?" Repeat the previous procedure.

Extension

Give students another copy of the story pictures. This time, have them make up their own stories for the same pictures and write a number sentence for each story. Schedule enough time for students to share their number sentences and the stories behind the equations. This will be the most instructive part of the lesson. Students learn best from each other.

Story Pictures

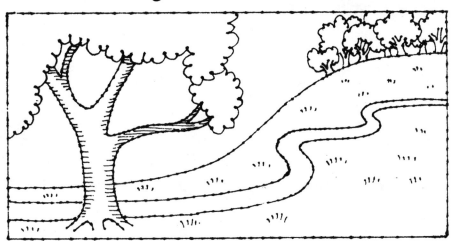

1.

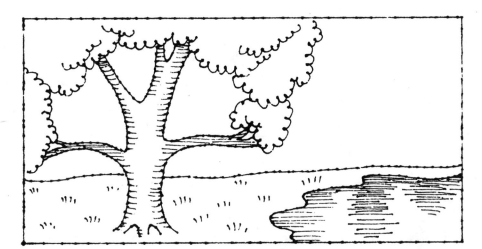

2.

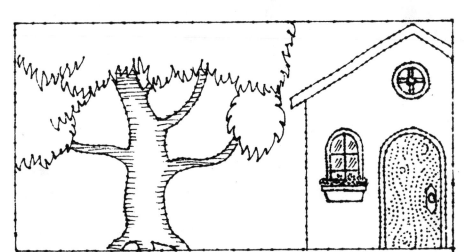

3.

Name_____

Cats

Half for You, Half for Me

Areas of Emphasis

- Number
- Mathematical Language

Group Size

- Pairs of students

Teacher Materials

- cats master (page 128)

Student Materials

For each pair

- 8½" x 11" paper
- self-lock bag
- cat pictures
- scissors
- crayons
- assorted objects (optional)

Introduction

This lesson offers students some practical experience with the term *half*. Sometimes we think students understand a term when they give a rote definition. We are surprised when they don't use that knowledge to solve a problem. This lesson will give them many chances to apply their knowledge of *one half*.

Procedure

Divide the class into pairs. Give each pair a piece of 8½" x 11" paper, a self-lock bag, a set of cat pictures, scissors, and crayons. Instruct students to work together and carefully cut out the cats. Tell them to store the cats in the bag. Then have them make a "Half Mat" by folding the paper into two equal parts. Discuss what the term *equal* means. Tell them to color each half a different color.

Say: "We found four beautiful cats near the park." Have student pairs get four cats from their bag. Tell them to use the half mat to divide the cats. Ask: "How many cats are in your half of the mat?" "Did you both end up with the same number of cats? Remember, you should each get an equal number of cats." Record the results on a table. Explain that mathematicians record the results of their investigations as if they were detectives. Use descriptive language as you model recording on the table: "We found

four cats. We divided them into two equal groups, and each group had two cats."

Continue with the following investigations and record the results on the table.

Say: "We were hiking on the mountain and found six cats. My mother said I could keep half of the cats. How many cats did I take home?"

Say: "My neighbor is going on vacation. I always take care of his cats. He has eight cats. I feed half of them in the morning. I feed the rest at night. How many cats do I feed at night?"

Say: "Carol works at the animal hospital. She saw ten cats this morning. She gave half of them shots. How many cats got a shot this morning?"

Number of Cats	Half Is
4	2
6	3
8	4
10	5

Let the student pairs have 5–10 minutes to make up some of their own investigations. You can use this time to assess students' comprehension of the material. Remind them to record the results so that they can share with the rest of the class. Praise good mathematical language. Store the cats in the bags with the partners' names on them. They will be used in the next exploration, "Graph That Cat!"

Extensions

■ After you have introduced this lesson format you can set up some investigations in centers. Place 10–20 of one type of small object in a self-lock bag. Make up several of these bags using a different type of object for each bag, such as buttons, large beans, lacing beads, clothespins, cubes, and crayons. Supply Half Mats or tell students to bring their own to the center. Have Task Cards made up for them to solve.

12 beads. My half = ___ beads

8 crayons. My half = ___ crayons

■ Have students do independent investigations at home. They should count a group of something and then calculate what half of it is. Family members should be encouraged to help. Provide a special spot in the room to display these independent investigations.

Graph That Cat!

Areas of Emphasis

- Statistics: graphing
- Number
- Mathematical Language

Group Size

- Pairs of students

Teacher Materials

- paper bag
- large sheet of drawing paper
- paste

Student Materials

For each pair

- cats in bags (from "Half for You, Half for Me")
- large sheet of drawing paper
- paste

Introduction

During the previous exploration, "Half for You, Half for Me," students sorted, counted, and compared cats. This lesson helps them organize the comparisons they naturally make. Tell students: "We are going to build cat graphs today, and I predict that they will all be different!"

Procedure

Divide the class into the same pairs as for "Half for You, Half for Me." Empty the cats from the bags into a paper bag and mix them up. Have each pair of students pick a specific number of cats from the bag. Ask: "Are all your cats alike?" Tell students to sort their cats into different piles according to type of cat. I recommend that you limit first-graders to ten cats per pair of students.

Give each pair of students a large sheet of drawing paper, a pencil, and paste. You should model every step of this lesson before the students work on their graphs. Tape your paper on the chalkboard so that everyone can see your demonstration. Show the class how to fold over a space at the bottom of the paper to form a base line for the columns and to reserve a place to label each column. Say: "I have sorted my cats, and now I'm ready to build a column of one type of cat." Demonstrate building a column of one cat type, starting from the fold line. Continue building columns with each type of cat.

Language and modeling become very important in this next step. Say: "This is where I have one cat in each column." As you say this, draw a horizontal line separating the first cat from the second cat in each column. Write a big number 1 at the far left of this row. Circulate as students make this first, crucial line. Model the next horizontal line: "This is the line that shows where I have two cats in each column." Write a big number 2 at the far left of this row. Continue until everyone has enough rows. Say: "Some of you might need more rows than I do."

It is important to label the columns so that everyone can discuss his or her graph without confusion. Have students suggest names for the different types of cats. As you decide the cats' names, write them under the appropriate columns.

Give the partners time to investigate and discuss their cat graphs. Give them an opportunity to share their graph with the rest of the class. "We have two Rita cats. We have five Fuzzy cats. We have three more Fuzzy cats than Rita cats."

Have students ask questions about the graphs. Ask: "Why do all the graphs look different?" Display the cat graphs.

Extension

Let each pair of students pick out two more cats. How does their graph change? Do they have to add any more horizontal lines? What new comparisons can they make?

Secret Ballot

Areas of Emphasis

- Statistics: sampling, data collection, analysis, and graphing
- Number
- Mathematical Language

Group Size

- 4–5 students

Teacher Materials

- 4–6 pictures of cats
- ballots

Introduction

Say: "The very old man had great difficulty deciding which cat was the prettiest. The cats were all beautiful in their own way," Display 4–6 pictures of cats on a bulletin board. I got great pictures from old calendars and magazines. Number them for easy reference and voting.

Procedure

Have the class list the attributes of one of the cats (such as striped, orange and brown, fat, long tail). Record the attributes on a piece of paper and hang it under the picture of the cat. Divide the class into small groups. Tell the groups to discuss and record the attributes of the rest of the cats. When they have finished, let them take turns sharing. While they do this, compile an attribute list for each cat to hang under the pictures.

Tell students it is now time to vote for the prettiest cat. Give each student a ballot. Form an election committee to sort, count, and record the voting results. Keep the rules at a minimum; it is interesting to observe how students regulate this process.

Have students use the ballots to build a bar graph. Form a graph-building committee to sort and build the bar graph. The rest of the class can use the election results to make their own graphs in groups.

Extensions

- Ask the class: "Do you think the election results would be the same if a different class voted on the cats?" Discuss this first and then actually arrange for another class to vote on their favorite cat. Discuss the differences in the election results. Why were the results different?

- Have small groups choose a cat and write an election speech for it: "You should vote for me because...." Have them present the cat's qualifications to the class or to another class.

1.
- striped
- orange and brown
- fat
- long tail

2.
- spotted
- black, orange and white
- short tail
- happy face

3.
- all white
- curved tail
- long whiskers

Fraction Mats

Areas of Emphasis

- Number: fractions
- Problem Solving
- Mathematical Language

Group Size

- 3–4 students

Teacher Materials

- beans

Student Materials

For each group

- large sheet of drawing paper
- crayons
- beans

Introduction

Say: "We are still dealing with cats! We have a lot of cats and a lot of work to do. We want to make sure that we divide the work as equally as we can."

Give each student a large sheet of drawing paper and crayons. Say: "We are going to make fraction mats that will help us solve some problems." Tell students to fold the paper in half and color each half a different color for easy visibility. "Use this side of the fraction mat when you must divide something into two equal parts." Show students how to turn the paper over and make a fold that intersects with the first line. Tell them to color each of these four sections a different color. Say: "Use this side of the mat when you need to divide something into four equal parts." Each student will then have a tool to calculate equal parts.

Have students practice using the fraction mats before they go into their groups. Give each student 12 beans and say: "Use your fraction mats to divide the 12 beans into 2 equal parts. Then divide your 12 beans into 4 equal parts.

Which is bigger: ½ of the 12 beans, or ¾ (3 of the 4 parts) of the 12 beans?" Repeat the procedure with 16 beans.

Procedure

Divide the class into groups of 3–4 students. Give each group a bank of beans. The groups will use the beans and their fraction mats to solve some problems involving cats. Do the first problem with the class. Then let students discuss and solve the rest of the problems in their groups. After each fraction investigation, let students share their strategies. Encourage them to use descriptive mathematical language in their sharing.

- The animal shelter got some kittens over the weekend. The shelter now has 20 cats. It has found homes for ¼ of the cats already. How many cats have a home? How many cats still need homes? Which side of the mat will you use? Why? How many beans should you use? How can you record your answer?

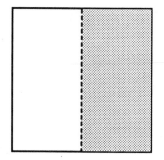

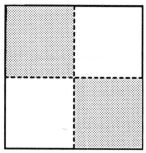

¼ of the cats have homes now. That means 5 cats.

¾ of the cats do Not have homes yet. That means 15 cats do Not have homes.

- Carla is an animal trainer at Animal Acts, Inc. She trains ¼ of the cats. She trains 10 cats. How many cats are there at Animal Acts, Inc.?

- There are nine female cats at the Perfect Pets pet shop. This is ½ the total number of cats at the pet shop. The rest of the cats are male. How many cats are there in all at Perfect Pets?

- There are 16 adult cats at the shelter for homeless cats: ¼ are black, ¼ are striped, ¼ are orange, and ¼ are white. How many are black?

- At Milo's pet store, there are four cat cages. The first cage has ¼ of all the cats in it. There are three cats in this cage. How many cats does Milo have in all?

Extension

Have students use their individual mats and beans for this extension. Say: "Which is more: ½ of 36, or ¼ of 60?" Have students predict the answer and check it with their fraction mats. Continue with more questions: "Which is more: ½ of 20, or ¼ of 36?" "Which is more: ½ of 16, or ¼ of 40?" "Which is more: ½ of 24, or ²⁄₄ of 24?"

MATH EXPLORATIONS BASED ON

Strega Nona

by Tomie de Paola

• •

A long time ago, there lived a woman named Strega Nona. Everyone in the town of Calabria went to see her because she had the "magic touch." She hired Big Anthony, who never paid attention, to help her with her chores. Strega Nona's belief that "the punishment must fit the crime" teaches Anthony a very big lesson.

Explorations	Areas of Emphasis
Three Coins a Day	Number Measurement: money
A Matter of Good Timing	Measurement: time Problem Solving Mathematical Language
The Pasta Path	Measurement: time, length Problem Solving Mathematical Language
Pasta Patterns	Patterns Number Mathematical Language
Tools of the Trade	Problem Solving Mathematical Language Patterns Number
A Weighty Issue	Number Problem Solving Measurement: weight Mathematical Language
Calorie Countdown	Number: addition with regrouping Problem Solving

Three Coins a Day

Areas of Emphasis

- Number
- Measurement: money

Group Size

- Pairs of students

Student Materials

For each pair

- variety of coins (real or fake)
- 100 chart
- variety of tools (such as cubes, graphing material, calculator) (optional)

Introduction

Say: "Strega Nona told Big Anthony that he would be hired to help her with the chores. He must sweep the house, wash the dishes, weed the garden, pick vegetables, feed and milk the goat, and fetch water. For this, Strega Nona would give him three coins and a place to sleep and food to eat."

Tell the class that Big Anthony appreciated Strega Nona's offer, but what did it really mean? What three coins would Strega Nona give Big Anthony? Would he receive the coins every day, every week, or every month?

Procedure

Divide the class into pairs, and give each pair a variety of coins. (If possible, provide real money; fake money looks fake and diminishes enthusiasm. In the 12 years I have had my coin bank, I have never had a student take a penny from it. If you are apprehensive, then set up a Check In/Check Out system; the group is responsible for the loss if one occurs.) Provide each pair with a 100 chart. It's a good tool to test the explorations. Remind the pairs that both members are responsible for their work.

Say: "Big Anthony's first day working for Strega Nona was disastrous. He overslept, was too late for breakfast, and hit his head as he went through Strega Nona's little door. At the end of the day, Strega Nona gave him three coins. He had only seven cents in his hand. What three coins did he get?" Tell the pairs to start investigating the problem. When they are finished, bring the class together and let pairs share their results and their strategies. Make sure a few of them illustrate how they used the 100 chart to check their predictions.

Now that the pairs are familiar with the format and have reviewed using the 100 chart, they are ready for another problem. "Big Anthony was getting used to working for Strega Nona. He almost never hit his head on her door, he always got out of bed in time for his porridge, and she never caught him napping under the fig tree. This week he mulched the garden, fixed the roof of her house, and collected the eggs every morning without breaking one. Strega Nona gave him 3 coins. He had 45 cents in his hand. What 3 coins did he get?" Again bring the class together to share strategies after they have solved the problem. Choose someone to demonstrate the coin pattern on the 100 chart.

Say: "Big Anthony is a new man! He gets up before the rooster, never naps under the fig tree, and always asks Strega Nona for more work when he finishes early. This week Strega Nona gave him 3 coins, a big smile, and a quick kiss on the cheek. He had 80 cents in his hand. What 3 coins did he get? Strega Nona tells him this will be his weekly wage because he is such a hard worker." Let the pairs share their strategies with the class. Choose someone to illustrate the coin pattern on the 100 chart.

Extensions

■ This activity involves using Big Anthony's wage (80 cents per week) and solving a problem. Supply each pair of students with a variety of tools such as cubes, graphing material, paper and pencil, and calculators.

Introduce the problem to the entire class: "Big Anthony wants to buy a book on organic gardening. It costs $3.75. How many weeks will he have to work to earn enough money to purchase this book?" Instruct the pairs to discuss the situation, come up with a strategy, and show their strategy to the rest of the class, either by choosing a spokesperson or writing down an account of their strategy. You will see a variety of approaches to the problem. Take advantage of the opportunity to listen to the interaction of each pair. This type of assessment is more meaningful than a test score.

■ Let students use a 100 chart and coins to solve the coin mysteries shown below. Students must record their work. They can work on this activity when they have extra time.

3 coins that equal 15¢	4 coins that equal 21¢	5 coins that equal 45¢
3 coins that equal 11¢	4 coins that equal 26¢	5 coins that equal 30¢
3 coins that equal 16¢	4 coins that equal 35¢	5 coins that equal 25¢
3 coins that equal 25¢	4 coins that equal 46¢	5 coins that equal 85¢
3 coins that equal 30¢	4 coins that equal 60¢	6 coins that equal 41¢
3 coins that equal 35¢	4 coins that equal 80¢	6 coins that equal 50¢
3 coins that equal 51¢	4 coins that equal 85¢	6 coins that equal 78¢

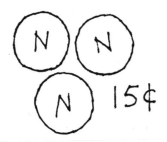

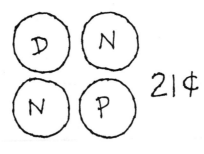

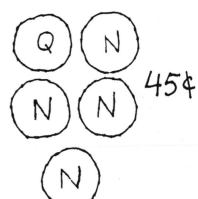

A Matter of Good Timing

Areas of Emphasis

- Measurement: time
- Problem Solving
- Mathematical Language

Group Size

- 4–5 students

Student Materials

For each group

- clock dials
- calculator
- counters

Introduction

Say: "Strega Nona hired Big Anthony because she needed help with the chores." Begin a discussion of the chores the students do and how long it takes to do them. Start a list of the chores that Big Anthony might do for Strega Nona and the time it probably takes to do them. Round the time off to increments of five minutes if you are concerned about the ability level.

BIG ANTHONY'S CHORES

Sweep the house	20 minutes
Wash the dishes	10 minutes
Weed the garden	15 minutes
Pick the vegetables	5 minutes
Fetch the water	5 minutes
Mend the fence	20 minutes
Wash the windows	15 minutes
Clean the pasta pot	5 minutes
Collect the eggs	5 minutes
Sing to the chickens	5 minutes

Procedure

Tell the class that Big Anthony starts his day at 7:00 A.M. and has promised Strega Nona that he will have all the chores finished by 10:00 A.M. "Is it possible for Big Anthony to finish all the chores on our list by 10:00 A.M.?" Students will have many opinions about Big Anthony and his

abilities. Let them give their predictions and reasons. Now divide the class into groups and tell them to find out if Anthony can finish his chores by 10:00 A.M. Provide each group with a clock dial that has moveable hands, a calculator, and counters. They may use any of these tools in their exploration. Remind students that everyone in the group should participate and that at the end of the activity they will be expected to share their strategies with the rest of the class. Insist that a minimum of 5–10 minutes be spent discussing the facts, the possible strategies, and the delegation of jobs.

The sharing at the end of a lesson is as important as the investigation itself. Students will see that there are many ways to look at a situation. They will also see that there are some strategies that work better than others in certain situations.

Extensions

- Instruct the groups to design a weekly schedule for Big Anthony. Discuss which chores must be done daily and which must be done once or twice a week. Let each group present its schedule for Big Anthony to the class.

- Have students list the chores they are assigned in their homes and design schedules that will fit their lives.

The Pasta Path

Areas of Emphasis

- Measurement: time, length
- Problem Solving
- Mathematical Language

Group Size

- 3–5 students

Student Materials

For each group
- unicubes
- 100 chart
- calculator
- meter stick (optional)

Introduction

Have students recall this passage from *Strega Nona:* "'Oh, Big Anthony, Look!' And pasta was pouring out of the pot all over the floor of Strega Nona's house and was coming out the door! 'Stop!' yelled Big Anthony. But the pasta did not stop and if someone hadn't grabbed poor Big Anthony, the pasta would have covered him up."

Tell students: "The pasta was traveling and growing at an incredible speed—every half hour, it grew three meters!"

Procedure

Say: "How many meters will the pasta path grow in one hour? In order to solve this problem, we need to review all the information." Write the word *Facts* on the chalkboard. Say: "What can you tell me about a meter?" List the information students give you. Say: "What can you tell me about a half hour?" Again list all the information students share. You are modeling a very important part of problem solving—brain storming and recording the pertinent information before starting to solve the problem.

FACTS

Half Hour → 30 minutes

Half Hour → ½ hr

Half Hour → 3 meters

60 minutes = 1 hour → 6 meters

Tell the class: "Big Anthony didn't expect Strega Nona back for another 12 hours. How many meters would the pasta path cover in 12 hours?" Now divide the class into groups of 3–5 students, and provide each group with unicubes, a 100 chart, and a calculator. The members of each group must discuss strategies and decide on one to solve the problem. They must record their findings so that they can share them with the rest of the class. When all the groups are finished, bring the class together.

Extensions

- Say: "Poor Big Anthony! The punishment must fit the crime. It takes Anthony two hours to eat 1 meter of pasta. How long will it take Anthony to eat the pasta path, which is 72 meters long?" Instruct groups to list the facts before they decide on a strategy. Schedule a sharing time.

- Take the class out on the playground and measure off 72 meters. Have students work together to find out how many feet, yards, giant steps, baby steps, body lengths, and jumps there are in 72 meters. Have them record their findings. Then have them use the information to make a graph.

Pasta Patterns

Areas of Emphasis

- Patterns
- Number
- Mathematical Language

Group Size

- Individuals in small groups

Student Materials

For each student

- variety of pastas
- glue
- 3" x 12" oak tag strip

Introduction

Say: "Strega Nona's magic pot made only spaghetti. We have a variety of pastas that would make Strega Nona trade in her spaghetti-only pot."

Procedure

This will be an individual project. Divide the class into small groups for easy management. Supply each group with a variety of pastas, glue, and an oak tag strip. I put each type of pasta in a self-lock bag to keep the pasta organized. Students will be curious about the pasta. Let them explore for at least ten minutes. If you do not give them this time of free exploration, you will have difficulty keeping them focused on your instructions.

When you feel that most of the class is ready, tell students to make an AB pattern. Do not have them glue the patterns at this point—this is a directed exploration. Let them share the AB patterns they have made. Continue by having them make additional patterns: ABC, AABC, ABBC, and so on. Ask students to share each of their patterns with the rest of the class. You'll be doing a minimal amount of teaching but a lot of listening.

Direct students to create a pattern of their choice and glue it onto the oak tag strip. Number each pattern and display the patterns so that all the students can look carefully at them. Have students try to identify the different patterns and record their decisions.

Extension

After students have identified and discussed each other's patterns, give them another challenge. Say: "I want you to choose only one kind of pasta and make a pattern using only that pasta." This will be difficult for some of the students. Say: "Make an AB pattern." Encourage students to discuss this first assignment with others in the group. Someone will position the pasta in two different ways, and word of this as a solution will spread quickly. Allow time for everyone to show and describe his or her AB pattern. Have students choose a different type of pasta and try another AB pattern. As students describe their patterns, introduce them to the appropriate mathematical language: *vertical, horizontal, diagonal,* and so on. Challenge them to make an ABC pattern using only one type of pasta and glue it to a strip. This time, they should write a description of the pattern. Later, read the descriptions to the class and see if students can find the patterns.

Strega Nona
by Tomie de Paola

Tools of the Trade

Areas of Emphasis

- Problem Solving
- Mathematical Language
- Patterns
- Number

Group Size

- 6–8 students

Teacher Materials

- stories master (page 144)

Student Materials

One per station
- graph paper
- counters
- calculator
- paper

Introduction

Strega Nona is a story filled with many interesting characters and incidents. It is a perfect vehicle to involve students in an investigation of problem-solving tools. Divide the class into four groups. Each group will experience a variety of problem-solving tools: graphing, using counters, creating T-Tables, using calculators, and drawing pictures. Set up a specific tool at each station and make a sign to identify the tool. The groups will rotate to all the stations.

Procedure

Give each group a copy of the first story and and read it with the students. Tell students to underline and discuss the important facts in the story. Then assign groups to the stations, and tell them they must use only the tool at that station to solve the problem. Then they must write a short description of how they used the tool and how effective it was.

Story 1: "Big Anthony was a hero. He scooped out pasta and filled bowls. There were 6 villagers sitting under the big oak tree. They each ate 3 bowls of pasta. How many bowls of pasta did Anthony serve?"

When all the groups have finished, have them go to a new station and use a different tool to solve the same problem. Continue until all the groups have used all the tools. Remind students to write a summary of the effectiveness of the tool immediately after they use it. Then bring students together to share their work. Direct the discussion to the positive and negative aspects of the different tools. Students will find that some tools were better suited for certain situations.

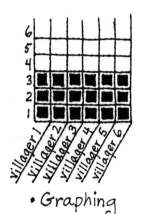

• Graphing

•Working with counters

Villager	Bowls
1	3
2	6
3	9
4	12
5	15
6	18

•Using a table

Give each group a copy of the second story. Again have them underline the important facts. Then assign them to the stations.

Story 2: "Strega Nona could cure warts. One morning, Big Anthony went out to get the eggs. He saw 3 men outside Strega Nona's door. They each had 15 warts. Strega Nona worked hard and cured all the warts. How many warts did she cure?"

When everyone has finished, bring the class together again and have the groups share the results and their observations. This time, direct the discussion to any patterns they saw as well as the positive and negative aspects of the mathematical tools they used.

Story 3: "Big Anthony took good care of Strega Nona's garden. There were more tomatoes than they could use. Strega Nona told Anthony to take 2 dozen tomatoes to the teachers at the school. When he got to the school, he didn't know what to do. There were 4 teachers. Anthony wanted to give an equal number of tomatoes to each teacher. What should he do?"

Stories

Story 1
Big Anthony was a hero. He scooped out pasta and filled bowls. There were 6 villagers sitting under the big oak tree. They each ate 3 bowls of pasta. How many bowls of pasta did Anthony serve?

Story 2
Strega Nona could cure warts. One morning, Big Anthony went out to get the eggs. He saw 3 men outside Strega Nona's door. They each had 15 warts. Strega Nona worked hard and cured all the warts. How many warts did she cure?

Story 3
Big Anthony took good care of Strega Nona's garden. There were more tomatoes than they could use. Strega Nona told Anthony to take 2 dozen tomatoes to the teachers at the school. When he got to the school, he didn't know what to do. There were 4 teachers. Anthony wanted to give an equal number of tomatoes to each teacher. What should he do?

A Weighty Issue

Areas of Emphasis

- Number
- Problem Solving
- Measurement: weight
- Mathematical Language

Group Size

- 3–5 students

Teacher Materials

- team estimations master (page 147) (optional)

Student Materials

For each group

- counters
- 100 chart
- graph paper
- calculator
- team estimations sheet (optional)

Introduction

Say: "Strega Nona returned just in time. The pasta situation had gotten out of control, and the townspeople were turning on Big Anthony. 'Now wait,' said Strega Nona. 'The punishment must fit the crime.' Big Anthony ate pasta until Strega Nona could get back into her little house. Big Anthony ate so much pasta that he gained a lot of weight. He gained ½ pound for every meter of the pasta path. The path was an incredible 72 meters. How many pounds did Anthony gain?"

Procedure

Tell the class they must calculate how many pounds Anthony gained. Divide the class into small groups. Tell students to discuss and list the facts of the problem, choose a strategy or tool, and then work together. Have mathematical tools available to the groups—counters, 100 charts, paper and pencil, graph paper, and calculators. Have students generate a list of the various strategies they used. When all the groups have finished, let them share their solutions with the entire class. Ask: "Do you think this was the best tool to use? Why?" Display the groups' work for everyone to see. It gives the class a chance to review each group's effort at their leisure and is an added incentive to do quality work.

Extension

Ask: "If you wanted to know how much Big Anthony weighs now, what information would you need to know first? That's right, you would need to know how much Big Anthony weighed before he had to eat the pasta path!" Tell students you will not simply give them this information; they will have to figure it out from clues that you give them. Give each group a copy of the team estimations sheet. Ask the groups to estimate Big Anthony's original weight and write it in the first box. Then give them a series of mathematical clues that will narrow the parameters of their predictions. After each clue, they may change their estimate and write it in the next box.

Clue 1: It is a 3-digit number that is more than 100 and less than 200.

Clue 2: All the digits add up to 9. There are only 9 possibilities. Can they find them all? (180, 108, 171, 117, 162, 126, 153, 135, 144)

Clue 3: All the digits are odd numbers. (That disqualifies 5 of the 9 possibilities.)

Clue 4: The number in the ones place is half of 10. (The answer has to be 135 pounds.)

Some students will feel they have the correct answer after the first clue. Insist that they continue with the activity and test their prediction

● ●

with the remaining clues. Discuss the team estimation with the class. Did their guess change
after the first, second, and third clues? Did they
have a difficult time understanding any of the
mathematical terms: *digits, odd numbers, ones
place,* or *half*? Did it help to discuss the clues
with the group members? Have each group write
a short summary of the math they had to use in
order to solve the problem.

Have the groups calculate Big Anthony's new
weight using his original weight of 135 pounds
and his weight gain of 36 pounds.

Note: You should divide the exploration "A
Weighty Issue" into as many days or sections as
you feel necessary, depending on your class's
attention span. Adjust the difficulty level by
changing the numbers involved—in this way,
you can do the exploration at any time during
the year.

Team Estimations

After three clues—Final estimation	After two clues	After one clue	Estimation

Names _____

Calorie Countdown

Areas of Emphasis

- Number: addition with regrouping
- Problem Solving

Group Size

- 3–4 students

Teacher Materials

- calorie chart master (page 150)

Student Materials

For each group
- calorie chart
- Base Ten Blocks
- calculator
- cereal boxes (optional)

Introduction

Before starting the lesson, write the following two menus on the chalkboard.

Anthony's Favorite Breakfast

4 pancakes
2 tablespoons of butter
4 tablespoons of maple syrup
orange soda (12 oz can)

The Healthy Alternative

bowl (1 cup) of oatmeal
1 glass (8 oz) of nonfat milk
1 apple

Say: "It is important to exercise and to eat balanced meals. Anthony has very poor eating habits. We are going to plan some healthy, lower-fat and lower-calorie meals for Big Anthony."

Procedure

Divide the class into small groups of 3–4 students. Give each group a calorie chart, Base Ten Blocks, and paper to record the meals. (If you don't have enough Base Ten Blocks for your entire class, then manage this exploration in a center approach.) Tell the groups to compare the number of calories in Big Anthony's usual breakfast of pancakes, butter, maple syrup, and orange soda with the number of calories in a more healthy breakfast of oatmeal, nonfat milk, and an apple.

Tell students to read the calorie chart carefully and use the Base Ten Blocks to calculate the total number of calories of the pancake breakfast first. Circulate and assist groups that need direction. Watch for groups that are not regrouping the singles into tens, and the tens into hundreds. Ask: "What can you do with all those singles? Is everyone in your group helping?" When all the groups have finished, have them share the strategies they used and the results of their explorations. Direct their attention to the importance of reading the calorie chart accurately, keeping organized, and checking their work.

Have the groups calculate the total number of calories in the healthier breakfast. Ask: "Did you have an easier time with this second menu? How did you change the organization of working as a team? Did you have to regroup this time? How many more calories are in the pancake breakfast than in the oatmeal breakfast?" Let students discuss and give an estimate for the last question. Tell them they may use calculators for this problem.

Extension

Have students discuss what they know about the role of fat and sugar in a healthy diet. Show students how to read the sides of cereal boxes for fat, sugar, protein, salt, and calorie content per serving. Let students investigate the amount in an average serving of cereal—usually ½–1 cup. Then let them write another healthy breakfast for Anthony. Supply them with the calorie chart, Base Ten Blocks, and calculators.

Healthy Alternative

Corn Flakes	110 calories
Nonfat Milk (1 cup)	90 calories
Yogurt (4 oz)	100 calories
Strawberries (1 cup)	50 calories
TOTAL:	350 calories

Calorie Chart

A
Apple	70
Apricots (3)	55
Avocado (½)	185

B
Banana	100
Bagel	165
Blackberries (½ cup)	40
Blueberries (½ cup)	40
Bread (2 slices)	175
Butter (1 Tablespoon)	100

C
Cereals:	
Corn Flakes (1 cup)	110
Oatmeal (1 cup)	130
Coffee	0
Cream (1 Tablespoon)	50

D
Doughnut (plain)	165

E
Egg	80

F
French Toast (1 slice)	140

G
Grapefruit (½)	45
Grapes (1 cup)	65

M
Mango	85
Maple syrup (1 Tablespoon)	49
Milk: nonfat (8 oz)	90
Milk: whole (8 oz)	160
Muffins: Blueberry	140
Bran	100
Corn	125

O
Oatmeal (1 cup)	130
Orange	65
Orange juice (8 oz)	110
Orange soda (12 oz)	180

P
Pancake (1)	162
Peach	35
Peanut Butter (1 Tablespoon)	95
Pear	100
Potato	90
Prunes (4)	70

S
Strawberries (½ cup)	25

W
Waffle	205

Y
Yogurt, vanilla (8 oz)	200

MATH EXPLORATIONS BASED ON

The Relatives Came

by Cynthia Rylant

· ·

The relatives pile into their old station wagon and drive over the mountains to visit their relatives. The reunion makes for weeks of hugging, music, good food, and happy memories.

Explorations	Areas of Emphasis
Visitor Graph	Statistics: graphing Mathematical Language
Guess or Count	Estimation Mathematical Language Problem Solving
Twos and Threes Around the House	Number Problem Solving Mathematical Language
Floor Space, Please	Measurement: area Number Mathematical Language
A Room of Our Own	Measurement: area, scale Number Mathematical Language

Visitor Graph

Areas of Emphasis

- Statistics: graphing
- Mathematical Language

Group Size

- Individuals in small groups

Teacher Materials

- large sheet of butcher paper
- map of the United States

Student Materials

For each student
- a small piece of paper
- tape
- graph paper

Introduction

Show the class where the state of Virginia is on the map of the United States. Explain that this is where the relatives started from. They traveled a whole day and ended up in a neighboring state. Ask: "Did you visit with any relatives last summer?" This can mean that they traveled or that their relatives traveled to see them.

Procedure

Tape a large piece of butcher paper on a wall. Divide the paper in half and label one side "YES" and the other side "NO." Have students write their names on small squares of paper and tape them in the appropriate column to indicate whether or not they visited with relatives last summer. Ask students who did visit with relatives to share a little of the visit with the class.

Say: "In order to read the graph, I am going to make some horizontal and vertical lines." First draw the vertical lines that separate the columns. Then draw the horizontal lines that separate the individual student responses. As you make your first horizontal line, tell the class: "This is where there is one of each response. I will write a number 1 in this column on the far left." Repeat with the second horizontal line. Then let the students take turns drawing the next horizontal line and writing the appropriate number in the far-left column. Have them use mathematical words to tell what they

are doing. Ask a volunteer to explain what the finished graph shows.

Have students copy the graph on graph paper. Have them work in small groups so that they can help each other.

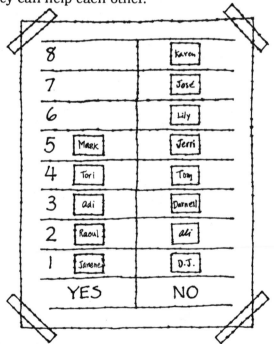

	YES	NO
8		Karen
7		José
6		Lily
5	Mark	Jerri
4	Tori	Tom
3	adi	Darnell
2	Raoul	ali
1	Janene	D.J.

Extension

On the map of the United States, have each student place a marker where one of his or her relatives lives. You may wish to have each student calculate how many days it would take his or her relative to get to your city, traveling at a rate of 350 miles per day.

Guess or Count

Areas of Emphasis

- Estimation
- Mathematical Language
- Problem Solving

Group Size

- Whole class

Student Materials

For each student

- calculator (optional)

Introduction

Tell students: "Large family reunions require a lot of preparation. Sometimes it is very important that you get an exact number to plan an event, and sometimes it is sufficient to make a careful guess. Making a careful guess is called *estimating*, and it is a very important mathematical skill. I am going to present some situations involved in a family reunion, and we will decide whether each one needs an exact number or an estimate."

> In grades K–4, the curriculum should include estimation so students can explore estimation strategies; recognize when an estimate is appropriate; determine the reasonableness of results; and apply estimation in ... problem solving.
> (NCTM *Standards*, page 36)

Procedure

This is a whole-class exploration. It is important that students share their thinking with the entire class. Say: "Pretend that you are preparing for a family reunion. There will be six guests visiting your family. There are four in your family." Write the following questions on the chalkboard and present them one at a time. Have students discuss the questions and decide whether an exact number or an estimate is needed. Record the responses.

1. What time will the guests get here?
2. How many blankets will you have to get for your guests?
3. How many pizzas should you order for dinner? What sizes?
4. How much oatmeal should you make for breakfast?
5. How many ski tickets should you purchase?
6. What time will everyone be ready to go skiing in the morning?
7. How long will the guests stay?
8. What else will you need to figure out, either with an exact number or an estimate?

Extension

Ask: "When do you use estimation at home or in school?" Let students work in small groups to discuss this question prior to writing their responses.

Twos and Threes Around the House

Areas of Emphasis

- Number
- Problem Solving
- Mathematical Language

Group Size

- Pairs of students

Teacher Materials

- floor plan master (page 155) (optional)

Student Materials

For each pair
- counters
- floor plan (optional)

Introduction

Say: "There were so many people in the house that they had to break into small groups of two and three for just about everything." Recall the passage from the book: "And finally after a big supper two or three times around until we all got a turn at the table, there was quiet talk and we were in twos and threes through the house."

Procedure

Divide the class into pairs. Supply each pair with counters. Tell students that you figure that there were 16 people in that small house after the relatives came. Their job is to find out all the groupings of twos and threes that are possible for 16 people. Instruct students to explore with the counters and record their findings. Tell them to stop when they have found a first possibility. Let each pair share its strategy for the first grouping. This sharing is very important. Students will learn from each other and might change their approach after seeing what others are doing. Do not recommend any particular approach.

When everyone has finished, bring the class together to share the results. Display the recorded work of the groups.

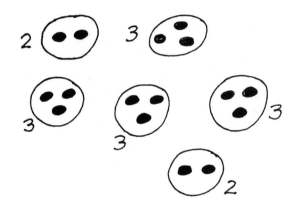

We have 2 groups of 2.
We have 4 groups of 3.

Extension

Give each student or pair of students a floor plan of the relatives' house and yard (page 155). Have students place their 16 counters in various locations. They are limited only by their imaginations. They can create any activities for the relatives and group them in any numbers. Have them write a short story about what the relatives are doing. Let students share and display their work.

The Relatives Came
by Cynthia Rylant

Floor Plan

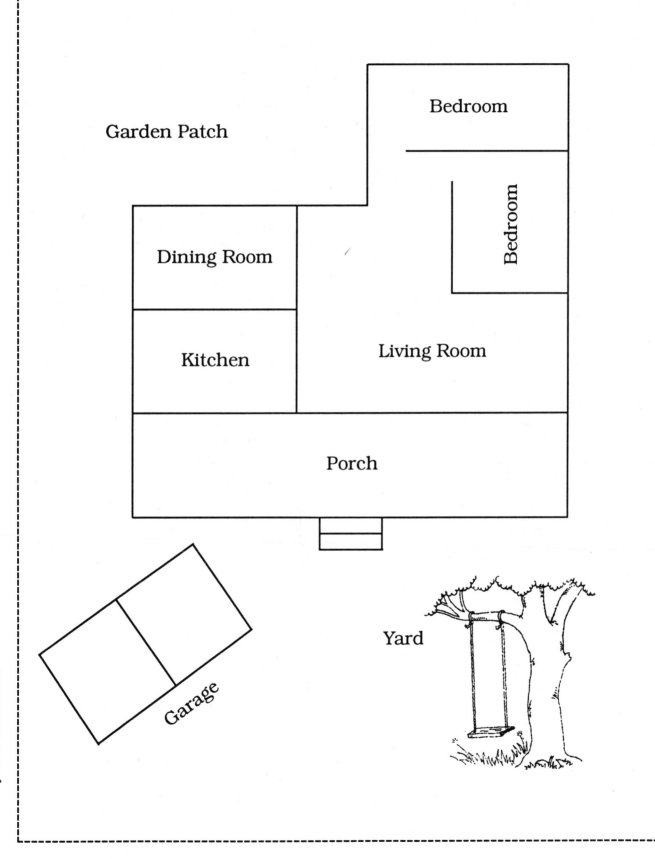

Garden Patch

Bedroom

Bedroom

Dining Room

Kitchen

Living Room

Porch

Yard

Garage

Floor Space, Please

Areas of Emphasis

- Measurement: area
- Number
- Mathematical Language

Group Size

- Pairs of students

Teacher Materials

- 1' x 1' pieces of paper (about 20 pieces)

Student Materials

For each pair

- 1' x 1' pieces of paper (about 20 pieces)

Introduction

Tell the class: "The relatives weren't particular about beds, which was good since there weren't any extras." Ask: "How much sleeping area would you need to sleep on the floor?" When I presented this to third- and fourth-graders, they showed me width and length with their arms. Introduce the terms *width, length, dimensions*, and *area* during this initial sharing. Show students a 1' x 1' piece of paper. Say: "This is how you measure space. This square is 1 foot wide and 1 foot long. It covers an area of 1 square foot. How many of these squares would you need to give you a comfortable sleeping space on the floor?" Record the estimates of the square footage students think they would need.

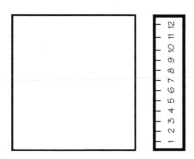

Procedure

Set this exploration up in math centers after you have modeled the procedure for the entire class. Emphasize that the sleeping area should be wide enough and long enough to give an individual student adequate sleeping area. As you set the 1-foot squares on the floor, instruct students to keep their squares in a grid formation. Show them how to calculate the dimensions and area and how to record the results on graph paper. Use the mathematical terms *width, length,* and *area*. After you have modeled the activity, have students work in pairs at the centers. Most of my students found that a 3' x 6' rectangle was sufficient. A few felt they needed more space.

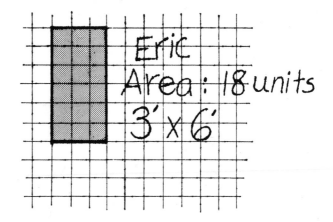

Extension

Set this extension up as a math center activity. Ask: "How much sleeping area would an adult need? A baby? A couple?" Require that students record the dimensions and area on graph paper after they build each sleeping area with 1-foot squares.

A Room of Our Own

Areas of Emphasis

- Measurement: area, scale
- Number
- Mathematical Language

Group Size

- Individuals in small groups

Teacher Materials

- 1' x 1' piece of paper
- 1-inch graph paper
- 1-inch tiles
- crayon

Student Materials

For each student
- 1-inch graph paper
- 1-inch tiles
- crayons

Introduction

This exploration should be done after students have completed "Floor Space, Please." Say: "We've done a lot of work finding out how much sleeping area people of different sizes need. We found that an average adult needs a 4' x 8' area, an average child needs a 3' x 6' area, and a baby needs a 3' x 4' area." Record this information on the chalkboard for students to refer to later. Include the dimensions and the area.

$$\text{Adult} \quad 4' \times 8' = 32 \text{ square feet}$$
$$\text{Child} \quad 3' \times 6' = 18 \text{ square feet}$$
$$\text{Baby} \quad 3' \times 4' = 12 \text{ square feet}$$

Continue: "Your next assignment is to divide a 10' x 10' room into sleeping areas. You will work on a scale version of the 10' x 10' room. The graph paper you will use has 1-inch squares. Each 1-inch square will represent a 1-foot square." Show students a 1-foot square and the graph paper. Say: "Explore on your graph paper with tiles to find your solutions." Demonstrate covering a sleeping area with tiles, outlining and coloring the area, and recording the dimensions and area.

Procedure

Divide the class into groups of 3–5 students. Give each student graph paper, tiles, and crayons. Encourage students to explore for at least ten minutes with the tiles before recording their floor plans. Remind them to refer to the chart on the chalkboard for the dimensions of a sleeping area for an adult, a child, and a baby.

When everyone has designed a room, bring the class together for sharing. I heard comments such as: "I need to redo my room because I didn't leave any walking space. I don't think people should walk on each other's beds," and "I forgot to put a door on my room."

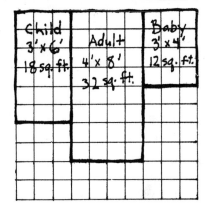

Extension

Have students divide a 12' x 14' room into sleeping areas.

Resource Bibliography

Professional Books

Baker, Ann, and Johnny Baker. *Mathematics in Process. Portsmouth, N.H.:* Heinemann Publishers, 1992. The purposes and conditions of natural learning are applied to mathematics.The emphasis is on unlocking the mathematical creativity of the child.

California State Department of Education. *Mathematics Framework for California Public Schools; Mathematics Model Curriculum Guide; A Sampler of Mathematics Assessment.* Sacramento, Calif., 1992. Documents that provide information to educators to help shape and evaluate their mathematics programs.

Commission on Standards for School Mathematics of the National Council of Teachers of Mathematics Staff. *Curriculum and Evaluation Standards for School Mathematics.* Reston, Va.: NCTM, 1989. Identifies a set of standards for the mathematics curriculum to help improve the quality of teaching nationwide.

Davidson, Neil, ed. *Cooperative Learning in Mathematics.* Menlo Park, Calif.: Addison-Wesley Publishing Company, 1990. Informative articles about many approaches to cooperative learning in the mathematics curriculum.

Edwards, Deidre. *Maths in Context. Portsmouth, N.H.:* Heinemann Publications, 1990. Shows the benefits achieved by adopting a thematic approach to teaching mathematics.

Stenmark, Jean. *Assessment Alternatives in Mathematics.* Equals Staff, Assessment Committee of CA Math Council. Berkeley, Calif., 1989. An overview of assessment techniques that promote learning.

Teaching Resource Books

Baratta-Lorton, Mary. *Mathematics Their Way.* Menlo Park, Calif.: Addison-Wesley Publishing Company, 1976. Activities that help the young child understand the relationships in mathematics through the use of manipulatives.

Burns, Marilyn. *About Teaching Mathematics.* Sausalito, Calif.: Marilyn Burns Education Associates, 1992. Presents a case for teaching math through problem solving and includes over 240 classroom-tested activities. Addresses topics that are basic to teaching mathematics.

Burns, Marilyn, Bonnie Tank, and Cathy McLaughlin. *A Collection of Math Lessons from Grades One Through Three.* Sausalito, Calif: Marilyn Burns Education Associates, 1988. Clearly illustrates the sequence of open-ended math explorations and how to be a "facilitator."

Cook, Marcy. *Think About It.* Sunnyvale, Calif.: Creative Publications, 1985. A problem for every day of the school year. Focuses on specific problem-solving strategies and skills.

The Diagram Group. *Comparisons.* New York: St. Martin's Press, 1982. A fascinating illustrated thesaurus of comparisons throughout the universe.

Downie, Diane, T. Slesnick, and J. Stenmark. *Math for Girls and Other Problem Solvers.* Berkeley, Calif.: Lawrence Hall of Science, 1981. Focuses on problem solving that requires logical and creative thinking. Activities designed to involve students and teachers in thinking in new ways.

Johnston, Susan. *The Fun With Tangram Kit.* Toronto, Canada: Dover Publications, 1977. One hundred twenty puzzles to solve. Solutions provided.

McConville, Robert. *The History of Board Games.* Sunnyvale, Calif: Creative Publications, 1974. Introduces classic board games and their history.

Richardson, Kathy. *Developing Number Concepts: Using Unifix ® Cubes.* Menlo Park, Calif.: Addison-Wesley Publishing Company, 1988. A comprehensive guide for using Unifix® Cubes. Contains hundreds of activities that explore patterns, more or less, beginning operations, place value, and more.

Ritchhart, Ron. *Making Numbers Make Sense.* Menlo Park, Calif.: Addison-Wesley Publishing Company, 1994. Hands-on lessons develop number sense and mathematical understanding—numeracy. Includes a chapter on authentic assessment.

Roper, Ann, and Linda Harvey. *The Pattern Factory.* Sunnyvale, Calif: Creative Publications, 1980. Illustrates the three levels of problem solving with patterning: manipulative, finding and continuing a pattern, and finding the rule that determines the pattern.

Stenmark, Jean, V. Thompson, and R. Cossey. *Family Math.* Berkeley, Calif.: Lawrence Hall of Science, 1986. Activities that promote problem-solving abilities in all mathematical areas.

Used Numbers: Real Data in the Classroom Series. Palo Alto, Calif.: Dale Seymour Publications, 1990. Each unit is organized into thoughtful investigations that teach students to collect, display, and interpret real data from the real world.

Stone, Antonia, and Susan Jo Russell. *Counting: Ourselves and Our Families* (Grades K–1).

Russell, Susan Jo, and Rebecca B. Corwin. *Sorting: Groups and Graphs* (Grades 2–3).

Corwin, Rebecca B., and Susan Jo Russell. *Measuring: From Paces to Feet* (Grades 3–4).

Westley, Joan, and Michaelia Randolph. *Windows on Mathematics Series.* 13 booklets. Sunnyvale, Calif.: Creative Publications, 1987. Simple, hands-on activities that address 13 different mathematical areas.

Bibliography of Math-Related Children's Books

Thiessen, Diane, and Margaret Matthias, eds. *The Wonderful World of Mathematics: A Critically Annotated List of Children's Books in Mathematics.* Reston, Va.: 1992. Contains reviews of nearly 500 math-related children's books.

Children's Literature for Further Math Explorations

Each book is listed under only one mathematical area. Most of these books, however, can involve your students in many mathematical areas.

Geometry

Carle, Eric. *The Secret Birthday Message.* New York: Harper & Row, 1986.

Ernst, Lisa and Lee. *The Tangram Magician.* New York: Harry N. Abrams, 1990.

Grifalconi, Ann. *The Village of Round and Square Houses.* Boston: Little, Brown, 1986.

Hoban, Tana. *Circles, Triangles and Squares.* New York: Macmillan, 1974.

Logic

Anno, Mitsumasa. *Anno's Math Games.* New York: Putnam, 1991.

Carlson, Nancy. *Harriet's Halloween Candy.* Ancramdale, New York: Live Oak Media, 1985.

Elting, Mary, and Michael Folsom. *Q Is for Duck.* Boston: Houghton Mifflin, 1980.

Lobel, Arnold. *Ming Lo Moves the Mountain.* New York: Scholastic, 1986.

Zolotow, Charlotte. *Some Things Go Together.* New York: Harper Collins Child Books, 1989.

Measurement

Adams, Pam. *Ten Beads Tall.* Sudbury, Mass.: Playspaces, 1989.

Anno, Mitsumasa. *All in a Day.* New York: Putnam, 1986.

Briggs, Raymond. *Jim and the Beanstalk.* New York: Putnam, 1989.

Carle, Eric. *Papa, Please Get the Moon for Me.* Saxonville, Mass.: Picture Book Studio, 1986.

Carrick, Carol. *Patrick's Dinosaurs.* New York: Ticknor & Fields, 1985.

Douglas, Barbara. *Good as New.* New York: Lothrop, 1982.

Gibbons, Gail. *The Seasons of Arnold's Apple Tree.* San Diego: Harcourt Brace Jovanovich, 1988.

Gibbons, Gail. *Sun Up, Sun Down.* San Diego: Harcourt Brace Jovanovich, 1987.

Kellogg, Steven. *Much Bigger Than Martin.* New York: Dial Books, 1978.

Krauss, Ruth. *The Carrot Seed.* New York: Harper & Row, 1945.

Krensky, Stephan. *Big Time Bears.* Toronto, Canada: Little, Brown, 1989.

Lionni, Leo. *Inch By Inch.* New York: Astor-Honor, 1962.

Livingston, Myra C. *Circle of Seasons.* New York: Holiday, 1982.

Lord, John Vernon, and Janet Burroway. *Giant Jam Sandwich.* Boston: Houghton Mifflin, 1990.

Morimoto, Junko. *The Inch Boy.* New York: Penguin, 1988.

Myller, Rolf. *How Big Is a Foot?* New York: Macmillan, 1990.

Shulevitz, Uri. *One Monday Morning.* New York: Macmillan, 1986.

Viorst, Judith. *Alexander, Who Used to Be Rich Last Sunday.* New York: Macmillan, 1989.

Williams, Vera B. *Three Days on a River in a Red Canoe.* New York: Greenwillow, 1984.

Zemach, Harve. *A Penny a Look.* New York: Farrar, Straus & Giroux, 1989.

Number

Anno, Mitsumasa. *Anno's Counting Book.* New York: Harper & Row, 1986.

Anno, Mitsumasa. *Anno's Mysterious Multiplying Jar.* New York: Putnam, 1983.

Asch, Frank. *Popcorn.* New York: Crown, 1987.

Blumenthal, Nancy. *Count-a-Saurus.* New York: Macmillan, 1989.

Carle, Eric. *One, Two, Three to the Zoo.* New York: Putnam, 1990.

Carle, Eric. *Rooster's Off to See the World.* Saxonville, Mass.: Picture Book Studio, 1992.

Carter, David. *How Many Bugs in a Box?* New York: Simon & Schuster, 1988.

Cleveland, David. *The April Rabbits.* New York: Scholastic, 1986.

Crews, Donald. *Ten Black Dots.* New York: Greenwillow, 1986.

Ehlert, Lois. *Fish Eyes.* Orlando, Fla.: Harcourt Brace Jovanovich, 1990.

Feelings, Muriel. *Moja Means One: Swahili Counting Book.* New York: Dial Books, 1971.

Hindley, Judy. *How Many Twos?* New York: Doubleday, 1991.

Hooks, William. *Dirty Dozen Dogs.* New York: Bantam, 1990.

Kasza, Keiko. *The Wolf's Chicken Stew.* New York: Putnam, 1987.

Kitamura, Satoshi. *When Sheep Cannot Sleep.* New York: Farrar, Straus & Giroux, 1988.

Mahy, Margaret. *17 Kings and 42 Elephants.* New York: Dial Books, 1987.

Mathews, Louise. *Bunches and Bunches of Bunnies.* New York: Scholastic, 1980.

Mathis, Sharon B. *The Hundred-Penny Box.* New York: Penguin, 1986.

Mosel, Arlene. *The Funny Little Woman.* New York: Dutton, 1972.

Munsch, Robert. *Moira's Birthday.* Buffalo: Firefly Books, 1987.

O'Keefe, Susan Heyboer. *One Hungry Monster: A Counting Book.* Boston: Little, Brown, 1992.

Rees, Mary. *Ten in a Bed.* Boston: Little, Brown, 1988.

Schwartz, David. *How Much Is a Million?* New York: Scholastic, 1987.

Sheppard, Jeff. *The Right Number of Elephants.* New York: Harper Collins Child Books, 1990.

Silverstein, Shel. *Where the Sidewalk Ends.* New York: Harper & Row Junior Books, 1974.

Pattern

Hutchins, Pat. *Don't Forget the Bacon.* New York: Morrow, 1989.

Polacco, Patricia. *Rechenka's Eggs.* New York: Putnam, 1988.

Yarbrough, Camille. *Cornrows.* New York: Putnam, 1981.

Explorations

Indexed by Area of Emphasis

• •

Measurement

Number

Patterns

Probability

Problem Solving

Statistics

Notes

Notes